Thomas Harriot

SCIENCE PIONEER

Thomas Harriot
SCIENCE PIONEER

by Ralph C. Staiger

CLARION BOOKS / *New York*

Clarion Books
a Houghton Mifflin Company imprint
215 Park Avenue South, New York, NY 10003
Text copyright © 1998 by Ralph C. Staiger

The text is 12/16-point Meridien.

Printed in the USA.

Library of Congress Cataloging-in-Publication Data

Staiger, Ralph.
Thomas Harriot, science pioneer / by Ralph Staiger.
p. cm.
Includes bibliographical references and index.
Summary: Examines the life and studies of the sixteenth-century scholar,
mathematician, explorer, optician, and astronomer, Thomas Harriot.
ISBN 0-395-67296-1
1. Harriot, Thomas, 1560-1621—Juvenile literature. 2. Science—Great Britain—
History—Juvenile literature. 3. Science—Great Britain—Biography—Juvenile literature.
[1. Harriot, Thomas, 1560-1621. 2. Scientists.] I. Title.
Q143.H36S7 1998
509.2—dc20 [B] 96-41842
CIP AC

CRW 10 9 8 7 6 5 4 3 2 1

Dedicated to

◆

JOHN W. SHIRLEY

◆

Extraordinary Harrioteer who spent his scholarly career
unveiling clues to the life and scientific contributions of
Thomas Harriot

CONTENTS

ILLUSTRATIONS

Portrait of Thomas Harriot

FOREWORD

THIS BOOK IS ABOUT A MAN who lived in England during exciting times. Exploration and innovation in thinking were revived for the first time in centuries. England was becoming an important sea power. William Shakespeare was writing plays that would be performed and read for hundreds of years. The Elizabethan era, named for Queen Elizabeth I, was in full swing.

Thomas Harriot was always curious about things he did not understand. His contributions were great, but he published little. This is perhaps the reason his memory and his accomplishments were almost forgotten after he died.

Harriot was well known during his lifetime, from 1560 to 1621. He was what we now call a scientist, although the word as we know it today was not then in common use. According to the Oxford English Dictionary, the word *scientist* was first used in 1840 by William Whewell, who wrote, "We very much need a name to describe a cultivator of science in general. I should be inclined to call him a scientist."

For the modern reader, Elizabethan speech and spelling have been modernized in this book. English spelling in the late 1500s was far less standardized than it is today, and Elizabethan pronunciation and usage were also quite different. They can make reading difficult. Occasionally a word or a statement is given as originally written, to bring you the flavor of the time. Otherwise, this story about Tom Harriot is in modern English.

Except for the report he made on his explorations in the New World at Walter Ralegh's insistence, and his last will and testament, Harriot's writings were not made available to the public. He did a great deal of scientific work and took careful notes which were never published. The notes are still being found and interpreted by modern scholars who in their lighter moments call themselves "Harrioteers."

Thomas Harriot deserves to be better known by the modern world.

R. C. S.

INTRODUCTION TO
SCIENTIFIC CHANGE

THE NIGHTLY NEWS ON TELEVISION now takes us to events all over the world and even to outer space. Putting a man on the moon was thought impossible only a few decades ago; now we are not at all excited about seeing reruns of Neil Armstrong jumping on the moon, saying "That's one small step for a man, one giant leap for mankind." Changes in our daily lives which have resulted from scientific discoveries do not surprise us at all.

When network television news broadcasts started in 1946, they were primarily newsreel film. Baseball games were broadcast second or third hand on radio as the announcer read a teletype-printed running description of what was happening. Part of his job was to recreate the excitement of the game as he read. Future U.S. president Ronald Reagan, even before he became a Hollywood actor, was known as "Dutch" Reagan and broadcast baseball games in this way over Station WHO in Des Moines, Iowa. Now we can watch the action of baseball, football, hockey, and fast-paced basketball games as they occur, with the announcers providing background comments, or what is called "color."

The twentieth century has been extraordinary for the quantity and quality of the scientific discoveries that have changed our way of thinking about the world. But it is not the first time in the history of the world that great advances in science have taken place in a short time. After a long stagnant period now called the Middle Ages, in which few discoveries were made in Europe, people became curious about the world. During this Renaissance, more and more intellectuals wondered what was on the other side of the ocean, in the sky above, and within the human body.

It was quite impossible for a sixteenth century scholar to learn everything that previous generations had known. Most of the university and monastic libraries in England had been destroyed by the year 1550. Contemporary universities did not teach much mathematics and science. In fact, mathematical symbols and diagrams could be considered icons of the devil, and so people who wrote or studied them kept them hidden. Even being suspected of being in league with the devil was dangerous. If the reader did not understand what was written, he could easily ascribe it to demonic influences and report the mathematician to the authorities. No one wanted to risk being burned at the stake for writing a mathematical formula.

There were few instruments to aid calculation, and every computation had to be done by hand with quill pens and homemade ink. It took a brave man willing to spend many hours of toil to become a man of science in the sixteenth century.

One such person grew up in a tiny village in Oxfordshire, England. Later, he was well known in Elizabethan England as an explorer, mathematician, optician, and astronomer. He taught many people a great deal about the riches of the New World of Virginia when it was still *terra incognita* (unknown land) to most people. His name was Thomas Harriot.

It was fortunate that young Tom Harriot lived near Oxford University. As a schoolboy he was considered a good scholar and he was easily admitted to the university, where he met many important scholars who were also curious about the world. At the university he made many contacts with well-born students and wise faculty members, who remained his colleagues and supporters.

Tom Harriot maintained contact with a boyhood friend, Tom Buckner, all his life, even though they were quite different. Young Tom Buckner was not a scientist, but he was included in the party that explored Virginia because he had been apprenticed to a mercer. Mercers bought and sold cloth, and knew about textiles of all kinds: woolens, linens, and cottons. Tom needed him to study and help describe precisely the clothing materials worn by the people native to Virginia. His adventures in the new found land were a high point in Tom Buckner's life. He was later very successful in business as a mercer, but he is best known to history as Tom Harriot's friend.

This book is mainly about Tom Harriot's contributions to scientific thought. Little is known about his life, but a small group of historians of science have studied the few traces of Harriot which have survived for four hundred years. Like detectives, they follow clues which they have found in dusty libraries and in boxes and even in canvas bags in castle cellars. They also meet to discuss Harriot's contributions and to write books and articles about his work.

In order to fully appreciate Tom Harriot, it is necessary to know a little about the England he lived in. It was very different from our world.

Queen Elizabeth I

CHAPTER 1

Queen Elizabeth's England

In the same year that Queen Elizabeth I was born, 1533, the Spanish Conquistador Pizarro executed the Inca of Peru. During her life many other things happened. Some of them:

1582 · *London's first waterworks was founded and water wheels were installed on the London Bridge.*

1593 · *London theaters were closed because of the plague.*

1595 · *The English Army finally abandoned the bow as a weapon of war.*

1596 · *The first water closet, designed by Sir John Harington, was installed at the Queen's Palace, Richmond.*

Tom Harriot's monarch was Elizabeth I. The queen was an absolute ruler. She could help someone she favored gain wealth and position; she could also sentence a subject to imprisonment or even death. As a young woman of twenty, Elizabeth herself had been imprisoned in the Tower of London for "plotting for the throne." Her cousin, Mary Queen of Scots, tried for many years to take the throne from her. In 1587, Elizabeth signed an order for Mary's execution. Elizabeth's opponents, or those who displeased her in some way, were in constant danger. She brooked no interference with her royal right.

Walter Ralegh

Not even the queen's favorite, Walter Ralegh, was safe. Most of us are familiar with the story of Ralegh's throwing down his cape to cover a "plash" so that Queen Elizabeth would not get her shoes soiled. Probably this never occurred, but it might have happened.

Ralegh needed the queen to recognize him, for he was a younger son of a noble family and had no hope of inheriting land or a title. The queen was an obvious source of support. Even if the cape story isn't true, there is little doubt that Ralegh somehow attracted her attention and pleased her, for she honored him with wealth and appointments. She was also a very jealous queen, and when he married without her consent, he lost her support and she cast him and his wife into the Tower of London. Tom Harriot's life was closely interwoven with that of Walter Ralegh. He remained a close friend of his patron Ralegh during his good times and bad.

Queen Elizabeth was a truly great monarch, and very willfully built England from the weak kingdom it was when she inherited the throne into a strong world power. After her death, Bishop George Carleton commented on the "weake estate of this kingdome at Queen Elizabeth's entrance. All the States about her were enemies. Friends none.

"King Philip of Spaine had been refused in marriage by Elizabeth; at first he disliked her, grew to hate her, and at last warred upon her. She tried to make friends with Henry II of France, but he also warred with England."

Carleton went on, "Spaine, France and Scotland were enemies. . . . The treasure was exhausted; Calis [Calais] was lost. Nothing seemed to be left to her, but a weake, and poor State, destitute of meanes and friends."

Yet she built a strong England from this beginning.

English Growth

Although Shakespeare is one of the best known Elizabethans, much else was going on that was reflected in the country's vitality. Other poets and dramatists were busy as well. The population of England grew about 35 per-cent during Queen Elizabeth's reign. In 1558 the population numbered 3.16

million. By 1600 England and Wales had 4.3 million inhabitants. France and Spain were still much larger and stronger, however.

Spain and Portugal were the dominant sea powers when Elizabeth became queen. They had expanded their empires into South America and Asia. English sailors were more timid, and many of them disliked leaving the sight of land.

During Elizabeth's reign, this changed. She deliberately encouraged and supported expansion into North America, hoping that the rich deposits of gold and silver which the Spanish had found in South America would also be found in the northern regions. In 1584 and 1585 Tom Harriot was a part of this exploration. Later, in 1588, when the Spanish Armada attempted to invade England by overpowering the English fleet, the Armada's galleons were repulsed. The English were very proud of this sign that their sea power was flowering.

Religion

It was dangerous to be a Catholic in England in Elizabeth's time, and many people suffered imprisonment because of their beliefs. Elizabeth's father, King Henry VIII, had outlawed the Roman Catholic Church, taken over its lands and treasuries, and set up the Church of England, which had no connection to the pope in Rome. Instead, the king (or queen) of England became the head of the Church of England. Nevertheless, there were still many secret Catholics in the land who preferred the old religion, and their families sometimes protected outlawed priests in their houses by hiding them in concealed closets called "priest's holes."

Catholic Europe adopted the improved Gregorian calendar in 1582. But Protestant England refused to follow Pope Gregory's lead and continued using the Julian calendar, established by Julius Caesar in 46 B.C., which was ten days ahead of the Gregorian calendar. Spain, France, and Scotland were Catholic countries. Their spies were thought to be everywhere and probably were.

Even today, the English celebrate Guy Fawkes Day on November 5 to commemorate the suspected Catholic "Gunpowder Plot," an attempt to blow up the Houses of Parliament during King James' reign. How much of the plot was the result of infighting among political enemies is still being argued. For many years, however, English children dressed up and begged for "a penny for the Guy," so they could buy fireworks.

In 1588, the Catholic countries attempted to invade England. The "Spanish" Armada was not purely Spanish, but was made up of 130 ships of various sizes from Spain, Portugal, and city-states in Italy and Spain. The records show that the Armada carried 123,790 cannonballs of all sizes. The invaders expected to frighten England so that troops could invade the English seaside town of Margate from the Netherlands. This "Holy League" of Catholic countries did not succeed and the Armada escaped, badly defeated. England remained Protestant and the queen was a popular heroine.

During this religious turmoil, the world of science was just coming out of the Middle Ages. What we now call the "scientific method" hardly existed. Alchemists were still trying to convert base metals into gold, and Harriot's teachers who were interested in science were thought to be conjurers. With them, Harriot tried to break the mold, and based his ideas on careful observation and clear logic. But even he was influenced by those who had gone before him, as are we all.

CHAPTER 2

Preparing a Scientist

THESE OTHER THINGS WERE HAPPENING

1572 · *Two thousand Huguenots were killed at the St. Bartholomew's Day massacre in Paris.*

1573 · *Francis Drake saw the Pacific Ocean for the first time.*

1578 · *The ancient Catacombs in Rome were discovered.*

1580 · *Czar Ivan IV ("Ivan the Terrible") of Russia killed his son and heir with his own hands.*

Tom Harriot's early schooling was limited. In the mid-1560s when he was in the English ABC, or "petty school," he learned only a smattering of arithmetic and letters. Girls left school when they were seven years old and were taught at home, if at all. In 1569 Tom Harriot and Tom Buckner went on with their other friends to the Latin grammar school.

Grammar School

Schools were usually in churchyards. Like all Elizabethan buildings, they were noisy, dirty, and cold. The grammar the boys learned was Latin grammar, for an educated man was expected to speak and write Latin. When scholars finished Latin grammar school they would have studied Latin for seven years, and were competent to speak, read, and write it. Latin was anything but a dead language, for an educated Englishman knew that he could correspond with an educated Frenchman, German, or Italian by writing in Latin.

After they learned all the elements of grammar, the boys made "Latins"—the translation of English sentences and phrases into acceptable Latin. The master usually obtained the material to be translated from books called *vulgaria* because they were written in the vulgar tongue, English. These are a few that the boys had to memorize:

> Sit away or I shall give thee a blow.
> *Amove sedem sinautem colaphum male addam.*

> I was set to school when I was seven year old.
> *Datus sum scolis septemnis cum.*

> The master hath beat me.
> *Preceptor a me sumpsit poenas.*

Later Tom Buckner wrote, "Tom Harriot had a far greater gift for language than I had. He enjoyed reading the writings of the ancient Romans, sharpening his language abilities through disputation and debate, and writing poetry in Latin. Although I can write in English and Latin, I think that there are other more interesting things to do."

The students also studied natural philosophy, based on the teachings of the ancient Greek, Aristotle. Aristotle's ideas had been accepted by the Roman Catholic Church as the basis for thought for centuries and were still believed by most educated people. Tom Harriot, always curious about the world of thought, questioned some of these ideas. However, since schoolmasters were licensed by the local Anglican bishop and the grammar school was housed in a church building, Tom learned at an early age that it is dangerous to question church doctrine, for his questions often led to punishment.

Harriot did well in his studies, but sometimes he looked at the master without seeing him. He was thinking of other things, and his mind escaped the classroom while he considered an answer to a different question or problem. To his annoyance, he found that teachers preferred their pupils to pay attention to their every word.

Tom was much more curious about how things worked than the other boys were. He wanted to understand the secrets his surroundings held. Tom always questioned why things happened. He didn't always get answers, but that didn't stop him from wondering.

Although he came from a poor family, on December 20, 1577 when he finished Latin grammar school he was easily admitted to Oxford University. His college was St. Mary's Hall, where the plebian scholars were enrolled. The neighboring Oriel College was for the gentry—the sons of knights and nobles. Tom Buckner was apprenticed to a dealer in textiles and so they were separated and no longer constant school companions. But although they were to live in different worlds, they were destined to see each other again.

The University at Oxford

Oxford University was small, but it attracted many extremely able or ambitious young men. Students were required to take an oath to wear only black gowns, for the fashion of wearing brightly colored dress had disturbed the school officials a few years before, and so all colored clothes were outlawed during the school year. This oath did not bother Tom, for clothes mattered little to him. In fact, he wore only black clothing in public for the rest of his life. Tom did not care to impress other people with his clothes; he had other interests.

Tom was taught little mathematics at Oxford, but he could attend public faculty lectures dealing with arithmetic, geometry, and astronomy. After the lectures he asked questions and discussed matters of common interest with the extraordinary faculty members who spoke at these public lectures.

Professors

One of Tom's teachers was Richard Hakluyt, regent master of Christ Church College. Richard Hakluyt wanted to become a geographer like his famous older cousin of the same name, who had written many books about geography and exploration. His lectures at Oxford were about the new geography, and Tom became his disciple and good friend. Among other things, Hakluyt was much concerned about the navigation errors of those who sailed on English ships.

Thomas Allen of Gloucester Hall was also a popular professor. Because of his interest in astronomy and new ideas, some unenlightened folk thought that he was a conjurer. His rooms were full of strange instruments and experimental equipment. One of his superstitious servants melodramatically told students that he saw "spirits" coming up the stairs to Allen's apartment "swarming like bees."

Tom was not surprised that some people might consider Allen a conjurer. Many strange beliefs were held by some Englishmen. Some of these were collected in 1669 by Thomas Brown in a publication called, *Pseudodoxia Epidemica, or Enquiries into very many Received Tenents and commonly Presumed Truths*. A few of these were: "Some people believed that the blood of a goat can make diamonds soft. Or that storks only live in republics. Thunder and lightning, some said, release noxious spirits which mingle with beer, wine and other liquors to make them poisonous."

The questioning Harriot was not likely to accept these bizarre ideas, nor was he likely to consider the spirits that were rumored to haunt Thomas Allen's stairway as real.

It might be useful to remember that in the early days of the telephone—which was invented in 1876—communication by telephone was also considered by some to be supernatural. "How can a voice be sent over a wire," some people said. "It must be magic."

Alchemy

An important part of Tom's knowledge came from the alchemists. Some alchemists were frauds who took advantage of the innocent with fast talk and large promises of converting almost anything into gold. True alchemists sought perfection in all things, especially in metals. Gold was thought to be the most perfect metal, and converting other metals into gold was the

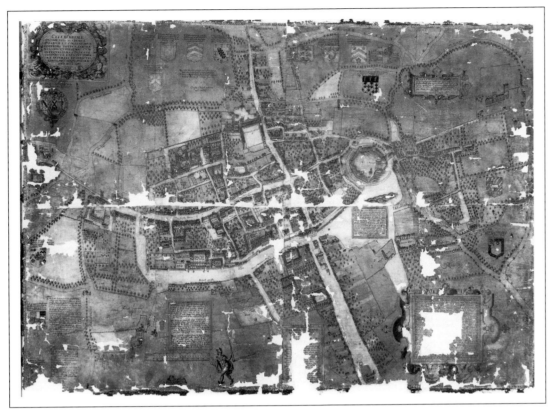

Map of Oxford, 1578

alchemists' objective. Such transformation was always of great interest to people looking for wealth. Kings and emperors always needed money. Many of them were secret clients of alchemists.

As a result, alchemists were careful not to give their methods away. When they wrote of their experiments they often left out important steps to keep others from duplicating their work. Today, some people accuse good cooks of doing the same thing when asked for a recipe!

Real alchemists were interested in what had happened in the past. They tried to unlock the secrets of their predecessors, so much of an alchemist's time was spent studying old alchemical texts. These early writers were presumed to know the secret, for instance, of how to use small parts of the magical philosophers' stone to transform a large quantity of base metal into gold. Tom studied the old texts for an entirely different reason: he wanted to know about the ideas they contained and their contributions to modern ideas.

In Elizabethan times, not all scholars put the old ideas of alchemy behind them. There were still many practitioners of the alchemical arts around, and some of them were held in very high regard by other scholars. John Dee was one of these practitioners. He was a mathematician, astrologer, sorcerer, and alchemist who was well acquainted with Tom, and considered Tom a good friend.

Another alchemist, Thomas Chernock of Combwich, spent much of his time trying to make the magical philosophers' stone. He wrote about the difficulty of keeping his work secret. The craftsmen who made his instruments and laboratory vessels were curious about them. Chernock stood over the potter as he created a retort and explained that his father was going blind, and he wanted to distill water to clean his eyes. When the joiner who made a strongbox to keep his instruments safe wondered what he was building, Chernock told him that it was a burrow for a fox, to be made secure with lock and key.

Oxford's St. Mary's Hall helped Tom Harriot develop his genius. But without his strong interest in observing and analyzing experiences and ideas, he would not have gained as much from his schooling. That he profited is clear, and not only in mathematics and science.

Some of his other Oxford friends were Robert Hues and George Chapman, who translated Homer's epics from the Greek. All were considered "good Grecians," competent in reading and writing the Greek language as well as Latin and English. Tom and Hues were asked by Chapman to read parts of his translations of Homer before their publication to ensure their accuracy. Tom told his friends later that he was gratified to be involved in this literary effort.

Chapman's preface to the first section of his translation of Homer's *Iliad*, *Achilles Shield*, was addressed "To my admired and soul-loved friend Mayster of all essential and true knowledge, M. Harriots."

Master Harriot

Tom had done very well at Oxford. He was one of only three scholars in his class who were awarded the bachelor's degree at the Easter Convocation, which had been delayed to July, 1580. He was then entitled to be called "Master Harriot."

When Harriot graduated, he had to decide what he would do to make a living. He could go to a city and open a private school, as some of his classmates did, but this did not appeal to him. Most young men without family wealth had to find a patron who would provide support in exchange for services.

Walter Ralegh had attended Oriel College at Oxford, but he left college before graduation. When Ralegh asked his former classmate, Principal Richard Pygott of St. Mary's Hall, to recommend someone to teach his ship captains mathematical navigation, Pygott suggested Harriot. After checking with their mutual friend Richard Hakluyt and receiving a good report, Ralegh invited Tom to live in his London household. Harriot had found a patron.

Tom moved to London in 1580, started a new life, and became important in building England into a world sea power.

CHAPTER 3

Ralegh and Navigation

THESE OTHER THINGS WERE HAPPENING

    1581 · *Russia conquered Siberia.*

    1581 · *Sedan chairs, carried by two or four servants, were in general use in England to transport the nobility.*

One day Tom Buckner wrote in his journal:

London, January 10, 1583: I was surprised to see Tom Harriot at the Thames dockside during a visit to London. We were delighted to see each other after so long, and stopped at a public house for a long talk. I had learned my trade as a mercer and he, in a very different way, had learned a great deal about modern navigation and the ways of Queen Elizabeth's Court.

Although Walter Ralegh has been in Ireland as Captain of the Horse to help put down Irish insurgents, he returns to London often. Ralegh is becoming very popular with the queen, and he makes every effort to improve his status with her. She granted him the use of a large

residence in London, and Tom now lives in rooms next to
Ralegh's own on the top floor of Durham House.

Walter Ralegh was ambitious and became an audacious contender for
power as he tried to succeed. He was handy with a sword, which was necessary for a gentleman in Elizabethan England. But he was also a reflective person who wrote poetry that was highly regarded by his friends and the queen.
He dressed well and knew how to flatter people for his own purposes. He had
an interest in the sea and seafarers' tales of adventure from boyhood on.

The Boyhood of Ralegh, *by John E. Millais, 1870*

QVID NON.

VIRGINL

Sir Humphrey
Gilbert

Sir Humphrey Gilbert

All London was shocked in 1583 to hear that Ralegh's half brother Sir Humphrey Gilbert had been lost in a storm at sea. A famous soldier, Gilbert had taken several expeditions to the New World. In the same year as he perished, he had established an English colony in the New World at St. John's, Newfoundland. Gilbert had been granted a charter by the queen for the discovery and establishment of another colony in the New World. With his half brother's death at sea, Ralegh became even more convinced of the need for Englishmen to solve the problems of navigation. He had good reason.

In 1578, Ralegh had sailed with Sir Humphrey Gilbert to the Cape Verde Islands and Africa. There were eleven ships in the fleet, and young Ralegh was in command of a ship named the *Falcon*. The ships in their fleet became disastrously confused on the ocean. None of the ship captains had any idea where their cohorts were. Afterward, Gilbert proposed to Queen Elizabeth that she sponsor a young gentlemen's academy for practical instruction "in navigation and other subjects." The queen never followed through on Gilbert's proposal, but Ralegh had vision enough to privately continue his half brother's idea with Harriot's help.

Mathematical Order Out of Navigational Chaos

In his room at Durham House Harriot conducted lessons in navigation. Sea captains kept Tom very busy. Many of those who called themselves "captains" were not really sailors but were wealthy gentlemen in search of adventure. They paid to outfit a ship, hired a real sea captain and a Portuguese navigator, and hoped to get a return on their investment. The capture of Spanish ships and gold was always a possibility. They would capture a ship by force, transfer its valuables into the hold of their ship or sail the prize to a friendly port. Although they were not called pirates in polite society, they in fact acted like pirates.

There is no doubt that both the actual sea captains and the "gentlemen captains" needed help in knowing where their ships were on the huge oceans. That was Tom's job. After he arrived in London, he spent much of his time at the docks, talking to experienced seamen about their work at sea. This was easy, for the River Thames provided berths for many sailing ships, and people enjoy talking about their jobs when they have a friendly, knowledgeable audience. Tom learned all he could about how captains used their navigational tools and how they dealt with their ships.

Many of Tom's interviewees were seacoast sailors who sailed from London to Plymouth, Liverpool, and other nearby ports, rarely losing sight of land. For the most part, they relied on the experiences of previous ship masters to help them in records called "rutters."

In rutters, the highlights of the water path along the coastlines were written down and passed from captain to captain. Dangerous rocks, shallow shoals, conspicuous landmarks, and distances from one place to another were detailed. Sometimes rough woodcuts were used to illustrate the rutters. Competent seamen also carried a compass for direction, an almanac to tell the stages of the moon, leads and lines for depth sounding, and tide tables for the area in which they expected to sail.

Tom learned the language of the sea from roaming the docks and talking to seamen. He took notes on skills such as whipping rope ends, splicing rope, and taking the kinks out of cable. He recorded how the officers and seamen on privateers shared their loot, and wrote the earliest known account of the names of ships' watches and the bells that timed each watch. He became an expert on the lore of the sea.

"The real captains," Harriot told his old friend Tom Buckner when they met in January 1583, "know what their problems are. First, the crude navigational tools they use are not dependable. When they sail for the Indies, they never know exactly where they will land. Second, there are very few maps and charts available, and those they have are often inaccurate. To make matters worse, some chart makers are not above misleading their competitors with wrong latitude markings. Sailing west by compass is simple, for you just sail due west following a line of latitude. But sailing north, or in a northwesterly direction is treacherous, for there is no way of calculating longitude."

Investigating the Past

To get comprehensive background information about navigation, Harriot sought help from his Oxford friends Thomas Allen and Richard Hakluyt. They lent him books from their private libraries. His connection with Walter Ralegh probably opened the doors of other private houses and provided access to rare volumes. Tom read or reread everything he could from the ancient world in Greek as well as in Latin. At Oxford he had read Ptolemy's book *Syntaxis,* which provided information about the ideas and discoveries of Hipparchus, who had first cataloged the stars centuries before. Ptolemy lived in Alexandria, Egypt, in the second century A.D.

The works of important Arab scholars were harder to locate. The Arabs had also used Ptolemy's *Syntaxis* as the basis for their astronomy, but they had made many improvements. The Syrian Al Batani, whose Latin name was Altegnus, produced astronomical tables in the ninth century that were much more accurate than those of Ptolemy.

Extremely important was the use of the Arabic number system, which introduced the zero and made calculation much simpler. Roman numerals were cumbersome for calculation. After Arabic numbers were introduced to Europe in the twelfth century, many, if not most, mathematicians used them. The Arabs also brought from China the secret of making paper, which made printed books possible.

Harriot's friend John Dee had translated Martin Cortes' *Arte de navigatión* from Spanish into English in 1570. This was the first textbook on navigation printed in English. In his introduction, Dee had emphasized that navigation was "an arte mathematical which demonstrateth how, at many times appointed, the precise usual denomination of time, may be known, for any place." A good clock with springs was necessary, said Dee, as well as hour, half-hour, and three-hour glasses. Tom wholly agreed with his friend Dee.

It was not until the nineteenth century that the chronometer was perfected. Dava Sobel, in her narrative of the long time it took John Harrison to perfect the chronometer, *Longitude* (New York: Walker and Co., 1995), showed how difficult it was for Harrison to have his invention, the first acceptably accurate naval timepiece, accepted by the British naval bureaucracy.

The Arcticon

In Tom's research he pulled together the investigations of the past and added his own ideas. His characteristically thorough approach paid great dividends as he developed a textbook of navigation called the *Arcticon*. The *Arcticon* was used as the basis for his course with the captains. They found it difficult, but being practical men, they could see the value of careful observations and calculations that would get them to the proper destination. When an English ship planned to make a long sea voyage, a sometimes untrustworthy foreign pilot had to be engaged. The captains, as well as Ralegh and Harriot, wanted this practice to change.

The *Arcticon* included tables and instructions for using instruments for sighting the sun and the North Star. It is very unfortunate that no complete copy of this valuable book has survived. Only the chapter headings exist, and they tantalize us to guess what Harriot actually taught his captains. Those headings read as follows:

1. *Some Remembrances of taking the altitude of the Sonne by Astrolabe and Sea Ring.*

2. *Of taking the altitudes of the Sonne or any stare by the crosse staffe with more exactness then hath been used heretofore.*

3. *How to find the declination of the Sonne for any time of the yeare & any place; by a speciall table called the Sonnes Regiment newly made according to late observations.*

4. *How to find the elevation of the pole, by Meridian altitude of the Sonne, & his declination.*

5. *Of taking the altitude or eleuation of the North pole by the North starre & a new rule of the guardes made and calculated according to praecise & later observations.*

6. *Of the manner to observe the variation of the compasse, or of the wires of the same, by the Sonnes rising or setting.*

7. *Effect of longitude on declination.*

We have an idea of *how* he taught these topics. At the end of his course, his notes indicate, he bade farewell to his captains with a piece of verse which suggests that he was not merely a dry academic, but tried to amuse his class with wry Renaissance humor:

THREE SEA MARRIADGES

Three new Marriadges here are made
one of the staff & sea Astrolabe
Of the sonne and starre is an other
which now agree like sister and brother.
And carde and compass which now at bate,
will now agree like master and mate.
If you vse them well in this your iourney
They will be the King of Spayne's Atarny
To bring you siluer & Indian Gold
which will keepe you in age from hunger and cold
God speed you well & send you fayre wether
And that agayne we may meet together.

Tinkering

Busy as Tom Harriot was in London, he still had time to play. But even when he played, he tinkered with mathematics. Looking out of a window in his room on the top floor of Durham House, he watched the drains carry water off the gabled roofs.

One rainy afternoon he wondered how much water was being carried off by the "leades and spouts." He measured, in pints, how much water came out of the spouts, and since he had no timepiece that would measure seconds, he estimated that each beat of his pulse took one second. In twenty-four hours, he finally calculated, 8.5 inches of water would have been in his 21.5 foot by 12.5 foot sleeping and class room if it had not been carried off by the "leades and spouts!"

CHAPTER 4

The Roanoke Voyages

THESE OTHER THINGS WERE HAPPENING
> 1583 · *The first known life insurance policy was issued, on the life of William Gibbons.*
>
> 1583 · *Ivan IV (The Terrible) died in Russia. His son Fyodor succeeded him, but he ceded most of his powers to Boris Godunov.*

In March 1584, Ralegh was granted letters patent (permission from the government) for a voyage to the New World. Tom Harriot helped him in selecting vessels for the journey, and by the end of April Captains Amadas and Barlow left on the two-hundred-ton *Bark Raleigh* and the pinnace *Dorothy* (a small, light vessel usually used as a tender or a scout). Many scholars believe that Tom went on the trip and returned on the *Bark Raleigh* at the end of September, having taught the two natives who were on board, Manteo and Wanchese, some English, and having learned a lot about the Algonquian language. But nowhere is there definite evidence, for no careful records were kept by the captains.

In late 1584, Tom Buckner wrote excitedly in his journal, "Tom sought me out today with a wonderful proposal. There is to be another voyage, and there is need for someone who knows something about cloth, so that the materials worn by the natives can be identified and studied. I have not seen him for almost a year. I think that he went on the long voyage to the new land of Virginia, named for the Virgin Queen, Elizabeth, for he was full of stories about the journey. We did not have much time to talk, but it did not take me long to decide to go with him on the next voyage. I am quite certain that my employer will let me take leave for this adventure."

Buckner made the necessary arrangements with his employer. The second voyage was scheduled to sail from Plymouth in April, and there was a great deal to do before they could depart. Harriot learned much about what he would need from his reading and the previous voyage. His responsibilities were much greater for this trip.

Sir Walter, Knight

The queen had knighted Walter Ralegh at a Twelfth Night ceremony in 1585 and named him Governor of Virginia. But headstrong Queen Elizabeth would not permit her favorite to leave the court. She was used to having her own way and he had made himself a valuable advisor. Even though he was disappointed that he could not join in the adventure, Sir Walter continued with plans for the voyage. He named the respected Sir Richard Grenville as admiral in charge of the seven ships, large and small, that were to make the trip: the *Roebuck*, the *Dorothy*, the *Elizabeth*, the *Lion*, the *Tiger*, as well as the two pinnaces which were towed by the *Roebuck* and the *Tiger*. Ralegh designated Tom to be his official representative and observer.

Tom made a list of instruments he would need for taking measurements at sea: several compasses, instruments for measuring the variation of a compass and the declination of the compass needle, three good spring clocks, and a ring to check their accuracy at noon of each clear day. The spring clocks of his time were notoriously inaccurate and needed to be corrected constantly by astronomical time with the ring. A universal dial, cross staff, backstaff, and accurate almanac tables were necessities. Other experimental instruments were also included. Tom thought of them as necessities, for he wanted to experiment whenever he could.

For recording observations at sea and for use on land at the end of the voyage,

Neptuni proles . qui magni Martis alumnus
GRENVILVS patrias sanguine tinxit aquas

Sir Richard
Grenville

he purchased a supply of parchment, good quality paper, quills, black powder to make ink, colors for drawing, a grinding stone to prepare colors for making colored ink, brushes, black lead for sketching, gum for erasing, brass compasses for scribing circles and measuring distances, and drawing instruments.

Tom wanted to have these available whenever he required them, and so he needed two assistants. Tom Buckner was put in charge of the writing and drawing instruments. The navigation tools would be in the care of a sailor.

Even after they landed in Virginia, Buckner kept his assignment as keeper of the writing instruments. He could use his expert knowledge of cloth when they described the apparel of the indigenous people, and Harriot knew that Buckner could write a clear hand. When they got to the New World, he would often dictate his observations to his old friend to save time.

En Route

On April 9, 1585 the fleet finally left Plymouth. Tom Harriot and Tom Buckner were on Sir Richard's flagship, the *Tiger*, with the admiral and other members of his council of advisors and adventurous young gentlemen. The *Tiger* had been outfitted by Queen Elizabeth and so had been made the flagship in her honor.

The Tiger

Ralegh wanted to please the queen to get her continued financial backing, for he was justifiably concerned that she was more focused on gold and treasure and was losing interest in the long-range benefits of the New World. The successes of Sir Francis Drake in capturing Spanish ships returning with their holds full of gold had made booty more attractive than exploration to the queen. Drake and Ralegh were strong competitors, and corsair Drake's ship, *Golden Hind*, was famous throughout England. In Spain, it was feared.

The Golden Hind

On the ocean, Tom Harriot and Tom Buckner worked hard. They took observations whenever the weather permitted and talked about the notes between observations. A captain on a huge ocean needs to know where his tiny ship is located and how to sail it to where he wants it to go. Tom used celestial navigation for the most part, coupled with common sense. It was a matter of using a few tools to locate fixed stars and calculating angles.

Early in the sixteenth century Pedro Nuñez and, later, Thomas Digges had pointed out various causes of error. Harriot therefore calculated a "Regiment of the North Star" in 1595 which was much more accurate. What Tom called a "regiment" we would call a "table of corrections."

Although it was easy to see the sun and the North Star in clear weather, making observations of them from a rolling deck was another matter. It was almost impossible unless the ship was becalmed. Foul weather and thick clouds also interfered with taking observations. There were lots of stormy days on a long transatlantic journey.

In order to determine latitude, Tom and his assistants measured the height of the sun at midday. They also compared the angles of various stars, especially the North Pole Star. The sun should be observed when it is highest in the sky, at twelve o'clock noon, and although their clocks were the best they could buy, they were rarely accurate to the minute. Consequently, Tom Harriot developed some useful tables for using the sun and the North Star in navigational computation.

On solid land, an observer can tell time very roughly when the sun is not obscured by using a *gnomon*, a vertical straight stick. Gnomon is also the name of the vertical part of a sundial. Its shadow moves during the day, and changes with the seasons. One can estimate latitude with a gnomon, for the midday shadow becomes shorter as you travel northward from the equator. An almanac to tell the dates of the solstices was important, for the shadow is shortest and longest on the days of the winter and summer solstices.

But the moving deck of a small ship is not a good place for using a gnomon. At noon, Tom sighted the sun by using a new invention, the backstaff. He had previously used a cross staff, which required the dangerous practice of looking directly at the sun. John Davis first described the backstaff in a book published just before the fleet departed, *Seaman's Secrets*. In it, he mentioned

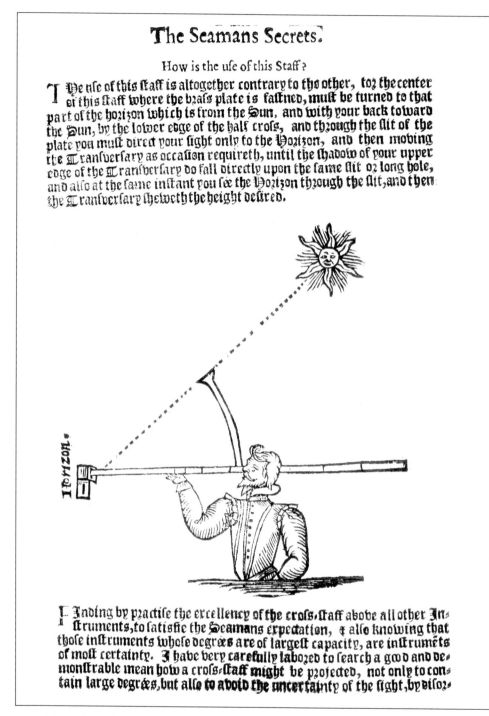

The Seamans Secrets.

How is the use of this Staff?

The use of this staff is altogether contrary to the other, for the center of this staff where the brass plate is fastned, must be turned to that part of the horizon which is from the Sun, and with your back toward the Sun, by the lower edge of the half cross, and through the slit of the plate you must direct your sight only to the Horizon, and then moving the Transversary as occasion requireth, until the shadow of your upper edge of the Transversary do fall directly upon the same slit or long hole, and also at the same instant you see the Horizon through the slit, and then the Transversary sheweth the height desired.

Finding by practise the excellency of the cross-staff above all other Instruments, to satisfie the Seamans expectation, & also knowing that those instruments whose degrees are of largest capacity, are instruments of most certainty. I have very carefully labored to search a good and demonstrable mean how a cross-staff might be projected, not only to contain large degrees, but also to avoid the uncertainty of the sight, by visor-

Davis's 45° Backstaff of 1595

Thomas Harriot as *"Amici Mei"* (my good friend). Tom was pleased that Davis had recognized him.

There were a number of experimental variations of the backstaff on board the *Tiger*. They had been purchased by the farsighted Harriot before leaving Plymouth. The backstaff is basically a graduated staff on which a sliding transom is fitted. Some people called the cross staff "Davis's quadrant." As the instructions on the accompanying illustration read, the backstaff is aimed at the horizon opposite the sun, and the transom is slid so that its shadow strikes the slit at the end of the staff. When both the shadow and the horizon can be seen, a reading on the staff shows the angle of the sun. An example of Davis's quadrant can be seen at the museum of the U.S. Naval Academy at Annapolis, Maryland. Many other maritime museums also exhibit early navigation instruments, for they were an important part of seamanship.

After sailing west from Plymouth the fleet made dry land at the Canary Islands. Tom gathered specimens of fruits, vegetables, sugar, ginger, tobacco, and pearls as examples of what might be in store in the New World.

On April 17, 1585 the fleet left the Canaries. Once again they were on the huge ocean. Time seemed to move slowly at sea.

Ten days out of Plymouth the crew had seen a partial eclipse of the sun. Tom was fascinated and took notes on his observations. Some of the men feared that the eclipse was a bad omen. Tom did not think so, for he knew what it was. The shadow of the moon had partially obscured the sun for a short time.

Log Book

Tom used a log on the *Tiger*. Captain Davis had just published the first log book in columnar form for English seamen and others to keep their records.

The first column of the Davis ship's log was for the month and date. The second was for the observed latitude in degrees and minutes recorded from the altitude of the sun at noon each day. A record of longitude was not kept, for there was no good means of measuring longitude. Next was recorded the direction (the course) of the ship, the distance traveled in leagues, the direction of the wind, and last, notes about the voyage. The compass variation was measured by using the North Star: "Pole Artick above the horizon."

The Seamans Secrets.

A Table shewing the Order how the Seamen may keep his Accompts, whereby he may at all times distinctly examine his former practises, for in every 24 hours, which is from noon to noon, he doth not only lay down his Latitude, with the Corse and Leagues, but also how the Wind hath blown in the same time.

The first Colume is the months and dayes of the same; the second is the observed Altitude, the third is the Horizontal Corse or motion of the Ship, the fourth the number of Leagues that the Ship hath sayled, the fifth is a space wherein must be noted, by what Wind those things have been performed; and the next great space is to lay down any brief Discourse for your memory.

Moneths and dayes of the Moneth.	Latitude. G. M.		Corse.	Leagus	Wind	The 13 of March cape S Augustin in Brasil, being 16 leagues East from me, I began this accompt.
March. 24	7	30	N. N. E.	25	East.	
25	5	44	N.b.E.nor.	36	E b.N.	Compasse varied 9 degrees the South point westward.
26	4	1	N. b. N.	35	E.b.N.	
27	2	49	N.	24	E.b.N.	Compasse varied 8 degrees, the South point westward.
28	1	31	N.easterly.	26	E.b.N.	
29	1	4	N.N.W.	9	N.E.	
Aprill. 31	0	0	N. b. W.	21	E N.E.	Compasse varied 6. deg. 40. min. the South point westward.
4	0	39	N.W.b.N.	15	N. E.	
7	1	53	N.N.W.	28	N. E.	Observation, the Pole Artick above the Horizon.
9	3	5	N.W.b.N.	30	N.e.b.E	
10	4	5	N.W.b.N.	22	N. e.	
11	4	45	N. W.	18	N.e.b.N	
12	5	16	N. W.	14	N.e.b.N	Compasse varied 7. degrees, the North point Eastward.
13	6	11	N.W.b.N.	23	N. e.	
14	7	16	N.W.b.N.	24	N. e.	

A brief

Davis's Logbook of 1593

Tides are important in influencing the course of a ship, especially when putting into shore. An unexpected low tide can wreck a ship. Tom recognized the influence of the moon on tides, and used tables in almanacs to predict the changing of the tides. In London he had already done this, but he knew that in Virginia he would have to take depth readings and create his own tidal tables.

A globe was used for great circle navigation. Sailors know by looking at another ship on the horizon that the earth is a globe, and they also know that curved measurements on a flat chart are likely to be inaccurate, especially for long distances. Harriot used John Holywood's book on spherical trigonometry, *Sphaera Mundi,* to help him solve these problems, and spent much time making calculations and drawing charts. He would later do much original work on the area of spherical triangles.

Navigation was hard work in the sixteenth century, and anything but completely accurate.

This is in great contrast to navigation today. Today, a hand-held Global Positioning System (GPS) instrument can pinpoint a sailor's position anywhere on

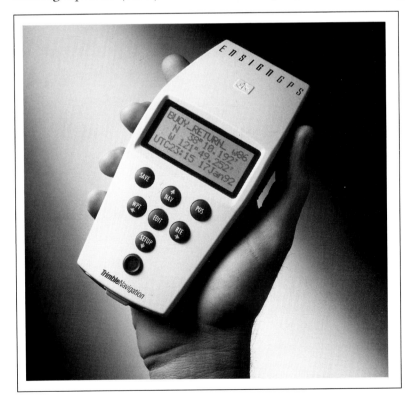

Global Positioning System Navigator

earth with the aid of a constellation of twenty-four high-altitude satellites orbiting twelve thousand miles above the earth. Using atomic clocks for extreme accuracy, each satellite continuously broadcasts the time and its position. A GPS receiver picks up these signals and, while listening to three or more satellites at once, determines the user's position on earth within a few meters.

Aside from sailors, hikers and campers can use a GPS device in the woods to avoid getting lost. Military units used them extensively in Operation Desert Storm in 1991 to pinpoint their location in the deserts. Some automobiles have them as an "option." How much easier Harriot's work would have been if he had a global positioning system device in his box of instruments!

CHAPTER 5

The New World

THESE OTHER THINGS WERE HAPPENING

    1585 · *Bartholomew Newsam constructed the first English traveling and standing clocks.*

    1585 · *John Davis discovered and named the Davis Strait between Canada and Greenland.*

    1586 · *Wheat, which the English call "corn," was in severely short supply in England.*

    1586 · *Thomas Cavendish left Plymouth on a voyage of circumnavigation from which he returned in 1588.*

Land Ho!

The first land the flagship sighted after crossing the Atlantic was Dominica in the Leeward Islands. Discovered by Columbus in 1493, Dominica was barren and inhabited only by a few Carib Indians. The flagship did not land but proceeded past Santa Cruz (Saint Croix in French) of the Virgin Islands.

The westward voyage had not been without incident. Shortly after they had departed the Canary Islands, heavy seas sank a small pinnace in a storm in the Bay of Portugal. The fleet was spread out by the storm, and the six ships remained separated until they met later at the planned rendezvous point, the Bay of Mosquetal in Puerto Rico.

Travel by land or by water was slow in Elizabethan times. When a possible treasure ship was spotted, there was plenty of time for the crew to bring up the light cannons, which had been stored in the hold, to their firing positions and open the gunports to get ready for action. No matter how crowded the ship, there was always room to stow away treasure that would be divided with the crew. If the prize ship had not been severely damaged, it could be sailed to a friendly port and sold.

Shipboard Rations

On board ship, the food was monotonous. Every man was allowed a pound of biscuit and a gallon of beer a day. The beer was a substitute for water and was much more wholesome than the water available at most ports of call. Each person aboard was allowed a quart of beer in the morning, one at dinner, one in the afternoon, and another quart at supper. Seafarers ate more meat than most Englishmen. On Sunday, Monday, Tuesday, and Thursday they were allowed either a pound of corned beef or a pound of salt pork with peas or beans.

Wednesday, Friday, and Saturday were fish days, and the men were allotted a side of salt cod or a long fish called a ling. Each week they could have seven ounces of butter and fourteen ounces of cheese. On Fridays there was no cheese for supper. The queen, in order to promote English fisheries, had declared that anyone in England who ate meat on a fish day would be punished. Since they sailed under the queen's flag, they obeyed. The men tired of their diet quickly.

Only the gentlemen had their own pewter or silver dishes, plates, and drinking cups. The crew ate like most people in England: trenchers of stale bread were their "plates," and they fingered their food off them. They usually ate the trenchers at the end of the meal.

First Landing

Everyone looked forward to being on land where fresh meat, fruit, and vegetables would take the place of corned beef, salt pork, and beans. Even the mosquitoes did not spoil the pleasure of eating fresh food on solid earth.

The *Tiger* landed on a small island off Puerto Rico on May 10, 1585. The next day the ship landed at the Bay of Mosquetal, well named for it was full of mosquitoes. Under the direction of Captain Ralph Lane, the crew erected a fort to protect them from the Spanish and by May 23 had finished building a pinnace to replace the one lost in the Bay of Portugal. There was a great need for this small boat to carry messages between the fleet's ships, and also to explore the depth of shallow waters.

On May 19, 1585, everyone was pleased to see the fifty-ton ship *Elizabeth* when it sailed into the bay with Thomas Cavendish, the young gentleman who had provided the ship and was given the title of high marshal. Now there were enough soldiers and men to defend against a possible Spanish attack. After a month, they departed Mosquetal with the newly built pinnace in the fleet and made a few stops along the way to Florida.

At Hispaniola they were entertained by the Spanish garrison. The English gave a banquet served on plates and complete with music. The Spanish returned the favor by furnishing horses for those who wanted to ride and releasing several fierce bulls for a hunt. All the bulls were slain. After gifts were exchanged and supplies bartered, the fleet departed. We can assume that the Spaniards in the lonely outpost of Hispaniola were simply glad to see new European faces no matter what country they came from.

In spite of the friendly atmosphere at Hispaniola, the English and Spanish were still antagonists. The next day, by a stroke of luck the fleet captured one small and one large Spanish frigate. Admiral Grenville sent the Spanish captives to nearby San German for ransom and dispatched Captain Ralph Lane to have the smaller frigate loaded with salt. Salt was very important for curing meat, and this could have been a profitable venture if Lane had not been frightened off by a few Spanish soldiers. Grenville was much annoyed with him, and they had ugly words.

For several days the fleet followed the Gulf Stream and sailed past Spanish Florida, constantly watching for Spanish ships. Harriot and John White, a gifted artist who was part of the expedition, also kept busy making observations of the coastline and making corrections on the charts of the area that they had carried with them. Unluckily, the notes they took during this part of the voyage were lost when the *Tiger* was almost wrecked. Harriot's notes, measurements of latitude, and the native names of the plants and animals they encountered in the Indies went overboard. From then on, their records were kept more safely in watertight boxes.

More peril was in store, for as the fleet approached Virginia the Portuguese pilot, Simón Fernándes, beached the *Tiger* on a shoal, and much of the food carried to sustain them over the winter was lost. This was a great blow to the crew. Now the seamen were dependent upon the food they would find in the new land. Fortunately they caught twenty pounds of fish in one tide, which showed that the area was rich in natural nourishment and convinced the crew that they would not starve immediately.

The *Tiger* was not the only ship that was beached or sunk in that vicinity of the Atlantic Ocean. In 1970, Dorothy A. Nicholson plotted the places where more than five hundred ships had been lost on a map called *Ghost Fleet of the Outer Banks*, published by the National Geographic Society. The *Tiger*, foundered in 1585 in what is now known as Okracoke Inlet, was the first of the *Ghost Fleet*. During the American Civil War, the Union ironclad *Monitor*, sometimes called the "Cheesebox on a Raft," sank off Cape Hatteras.

In World Wars I and II, German U-boats lurked off the same shore and torpedoed freighters and tankers. They were so bold that German sailors sometimes rowed ashore in the evening to attend local movie theaters. One German sailor who did not make it back to his submarine was found, drowned, with the ticket stubs in his pocket.

John White

Naturalists and explorers of the Elizabethan era profited from color sketches and paintings of the strange and wonderful things they saw, for there were no cameras or photographers in the sixteenth century. The expedition was fortunate to include John White in its group. Tom (or Master Harriot, as he was called by the rest of the crew, even though he functioned amicably with even the lowest-ranked crew member) and John White started to write and draw long before the landing on Roanoke Island. Harriot took depth soundings along the coastline, and White drew the outline of the shoreline. One of the first things Harriot did when they went ashore on a sandy beach was to try to locate exactly where they were, according to the sun and the stars. He always felt better after doing that chore.

On June 30, 1585, the fleet finally anchored at Roanoke Island and Harriot and White outlined plans for a survey of the mainland. They were well prepared by their West Indies explorations and their many discussions during the long voyage.

"*The arrival of the Englishemen in Virginia.*"

The survey of the area kept the team very busy. They developed maps, took hundreds of measurements, sounded the depth of bays and streams, and calculated the height of hills. These notes and sketches would become a very important record of the voyage of discovery and would prove valuable in informing people about the New World. The survey maps drawn by John White were the basis for most European maps of the region for eighty years.

The Natives

On July 3 a small party was sent to formally announce the fleet's arrival to King Wingina on Roanoke Island. Two days later Manteo and John Arundel made an exploratory trip to the mainland. These were the first of a series of peaceful visits to the native population.

White and Harriot were very interested in the Indian village and the people who lived there. They learned that the partial eclipse they had seen just out of Plymouth had been a total eclipse in Virginia. The inhabitants of the village had been frightened, and some looked upon it as a portent of the arrival of the fleet. Therefore they had not been overly surprised when they saw the English ships.

White made drawings of the village buildings and, later when he got to know them better, he drew and painted the women and men in their unusual clothing. Harriot dictated descriptions and observations until Tom Buckner's writing hand got tired and his fingers black with ink. When Harriot described things that he knew in England, he used English words, but native animals, trees, fruits, and plants were named in the indigenous language.

Recording Speech Sounds

The language of the people of Virginia was *Algonquian*. In order to learn it, Harriot devised a system of recording the sounds of the language on paper, together with the meaning of the words. He discarded the English alphabet, which has no systematic, definite way of representing all sounds. In the English of the time, words, and especially names, could be spelled in many ways. It was really "invented spelling," created on the spot by the writer with the expectation that the reader could figure out what was meant. Tom Buckner's name could be spelled "Buchner" and "Bookener," and often was. Harriot's name was often spelled "Harriot," "Harriott," or "Herriot." Sir Walter Ralegh's name was spelled "Raleigh" or "Rawley" by some people, but after he came of age he always signed it "Ralegh."

VOWELS

POSITION	FRONT			CENTRAL			BACK		
HIGH	i	(b<u>ee</u>t)	↲	ai	(b<u>i</u>te)	ȝ	u	(b<u>oo</u>t)	𝓮
	I	(b<u>i</u>t)	ε				U	(b<u>oo</u>k)	(z)
MID	e	(b<u>ai</u>t)	𝓮	ə	(b<u>u</u>t)	(z)	o	(b<u>oa</u>t)	ʒ
	ɛ	(b<u>e</u>t)	𝓵						
LOW	æ	(b<u>a</u>t)	2	a	(b<u>o</u>ther)	ʃ	ɔ	(b<u>a</u>ll)	ʃ

CONSONANTS

		BILABIAL	LABIO-DENTAL	INTER-DENTAL	ALVEOLAR	ALVEO-PALATAL	VELAR	GLOTTAL
STOPS	Vl	p			t		k	
	Vd	b			d		g	
FRICATIVES	Vl		f	θ	s	š		h
	Vd		v	ð	z	ž		
AFFRICATES	Vl					č		
	Vd					ǰ		
NASALS		m			n		ŋ	
LATERAL					l			
GLIDES					r	y	w	

Harriot's Phonetic Alphabet

Harriot approached the recording of speech sounds with his usual thoroughness. He studied the mechanics of sound production by the vocal cords and the placement of the tongue and lips, and he used algebraic symbols to represent the various sounds. Tom was careful to be accurate in his perception of the sounds. The two Algonquian natives, Manteo and Wanchese, who had been brought to England in 1584, gave him much help with his dictionary of Algonquian words. Their names were written by Tom as:

 and

In July 1585 expeditions to the surrounding mainland areas were undertaken, and the explorers were constantly drawing, observing, and making notes. It was exciting when they met strange native travelers, for they never knew what would happen. Harriot had a pleasant way with new people. He approached them with open arms to show that he was not armed. The party sat down, and Harriot showed them his writing tools and compasses, and what could be done with them. This always interested the new acquaintances. Then Tom asked them their names, where they were from, and how their families fared. He also asked them the names of various plants and animals. After a pleasant visit both groups said good–bye and continued their travels. Tom Buckner kept busy taking notes while they were talking.

The notes Harriot and Buckner took on these expeditions were meant to be technical observations, but they also had another purpose. Ralegh wanted the queen to know how valuable her lands in Virginia were, in hope that she would continue to support exploration and colonization with ships and money.

Harriot and Buckner's notes and White's drawings later created great interest on the entire continent of Europe as well as on the part of the queen and her subjects in England.

CHAPTER 6

Exploring Virginia

THESE OTHER THINGS WERE HAPPENING

> 1585 · *Lucas Janszoon Waghearon published* Mirror of Seafaring *in Holland, a book of sailing directions.*
> 1586 · *Pope Sixtus V promised financial aid to send the Spanish Armada against England. The Church was very concerned about the continuation of Protestantism in England.*

Tom Harriot is credited with bringing the seeds of science to America in the first chapter of Bernard Jaffe's *Men of Science in America: The Role of Science in the Growth of Our Country*. The chapter title was, of course, "Thomas Harriot (1560–1621)" and it highlighted Tom's important observations in Virginia.

Harriot's was not the first exploration of America, for John Cabot and Martin Frobisher had searched for the Northwest Passage in what is now Canada. An iron mine had been established, but did not last long, for gold and silver were the minerals most valued by the explorers. But Harriot's observations were an eye opener for most Europeans, who had no idea of what the New World contained.

Harriot's careful description of Virginia, its inhabitants and flora and fauna, was unique. He was interested in the possibility of mineral riches to encourage the queen to support future voyages and settlements, but he also described riches that could support daily life. The exploration of Virginia was mostly a scientific exploration for Tom, not just an adventure. But it was an adventure, too.

In late July the native prince Manteo, who had been taken to see the queen in England in 1584, brought Granganemeo, the brother of King Wingina, on board the *Tiger*. Granganemeo offered the hospitality of the island of Roanoke as headquarters of the colony. This was good news, for the visitors could now have a place to live on land and continue exploring.

Travelers naturally compare what they see with familiar sights at home. At least that is what Tom Buckner did. He compared the people, the trees, and everything else with those in England. Tom Harriot probably did the same, but being a scholar, he also used careful methods of observation and recording to examine what he saw.

The Native People

The Algonquians, Harriot found, were a peaceful people. They did not have any arms of warfare, nor did they have metal-edge tools or weapons of iron or steel. Their bows were made of witch hazel and their arrows of reeds. Their weapons were used for hunting food rather than warfare. The people lived in small towns, usually near the seacoast. The houses were made of small poles tied together at the top and roofed with bark or mats made of rushes.

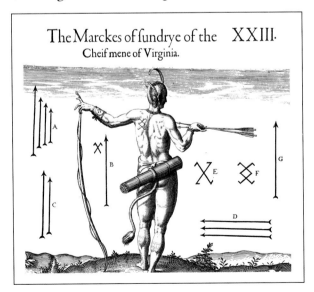

"The Marckes of Sundrye of the Cheif mene of Virginia."

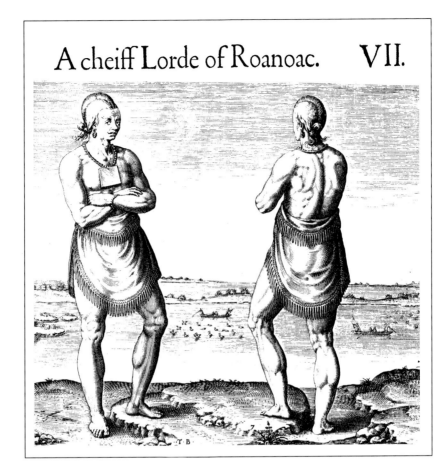

"A cheiff Lorde of Roanoac."

The chief, who sometimes also served as a priest, was called a *wiroan*. Usually a chief had one town in his domain, but some chiefs had more than one. The most powerful wiroan Harriot found governed eighteen towns.

Clothing

Since Buckner was a mercer, he was most interested in the clothing of the local people. Buckner noticed that deerskin was the most prevalent dress for both men and women. It was worn fur side in or was dressed like chamois. In either case, the skin was soft and flexible. Both men and women wore loose mantles and aprons tied around their middles. Their dress varied, and John White had a good time drawing and painting the variety of their clothing.

An ageed manne in his winter
garment.

"An ageed manne in his winter garment."

There were many deer in the area, and the supply of deerskin seemed inexhaustible. Likewise, the skins of other fur-bearing animals were used for lining capes to add warmth in winter. Otter, marten, mink, squirrel, and civet cat (skunk, which Tom said he needed no eyes to observe) were easy to bag on Roanoke Island. Black bear skins were used as rugs.

Dyes for deerskins and rushes, and even for coloring the people's hair, were made from various roots and plants. Red coloring came from the seed of an herb called *wasebur* in the Indian tongue, from small roots called *chappacor*, and from the bark of a tree, *tangomockonomindge*. In England, black dyes and leather tanning dyes were made from sumac (or shoemake), which was also found on Roanoke Island. Harriot realized that woad, a plant yielding basic blue indigo dye, which England did not have enough space to grow, could also be planted in the New World. Eventually indigo became a valuable cash crop for European settlers in the Virginia area.

"*A weroan or great Lorde of Virginia.*"

"On of the Religeous men in the towne of Secota."

Spiritual Beliefs

The native religion was of great interest to Tom. He found that they had many gods, but only one chief god named *Mantoac*, who created the world and everything in it. The gods had human shape; one single god was called a *Kewas* and plural gods were called *kewasowok*. Their images were placed in temples called *machicomuck*. The sunset, called *popogusso*, they believed burned constantly, and that bad persons went there when they died. As a matter of duty, Tom read the Bible to the natives and urged them to become Christians.

When the ancient *wiroan* with whom the expedition lived was sick, Harriot prayed over him, and he reported that the people were glad for his help. When a drought threatened their crops, Harriot prayed for rain. When the natives gave thanks because they had escaped danger or wanted to celebrate in prayer they made a big fire, sang, and shook gourd rattles. Tom was invited to pray with them.

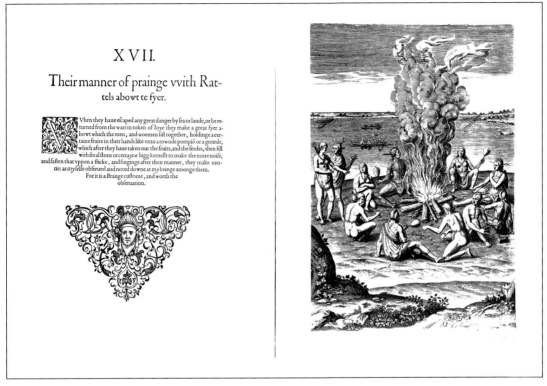

"Their manner of prainge vvith Rattels abowt te fyer."

Commercial Goods

Many products promised profit in broad commerce for the English market. The queen was much interested in pearls, and one sailor in the company gathered about five thousand pearls from the natives. He was an expert on pearls, and made several strings to be taken home as evidence, matching the pearls according to color and size.

The people wore silver and copper decorations, which came from upriver tribes. Harriot learned to his amazement that only one word was used in the Algonquian language for metal, gold, and copper. The company set up a rude laboratory for Joachim Ganz, the jewelry specialist, to test metals and possible gemstones. The explorers were satisfied that much commerce would result from the minerals they expected to find.

Cedar wood, which could be used for making chests, furniture, and musical instruments, abounded. Pitch, tar, and turpentine were plentiful and especially useful for shipbuilding.

Tom recognized the need for specialized help in determining which apothecary drugs could be derived from some of the plants and trees that the native people used. Naturally, he took samples of these unfamiliar medicines home. Sassafras, which Harriot had found in the West Indies, was used by the natives as a blood tonic. It was also used as a thickener when cooking soups and stews. In England it was later advertised as a valuable medicine for many ills, including fevers, broken bones, and falling hair. This valuable commodity was easily found in Virginia. A few years later Captain John Smith made a fortune sending shiploads of sassafras root to England from Jamestown. Captain Smith also described a more objectionable New World plant—poison ivy.

Uppowoc, which the Spaniards called tobacco, was dried and sprinkled on fires for ceremonial purposes and to pacify the gods. The smoke also appeared to have medicinal qualities. To early observers, it seemed to preserve health, for the indigenous people knew few diseases such as were known in England. Harriot reported that *uppowoc* opened the pores and passages of the body, and that he would take some home. *Uppowoc,* he thought, was likely to become a valuable trade commodity. This turned out to be true.

Wapieh, a fine clay, was plentiful. It was used by the people as medicine for the cure of sores and wounds. Pipes made from it also made good smoking pipes. Eventually many ships bearing tobacco plied between Europe and Virginia. Years later Tom Harriot suffered great agony from a cancer in his nose. He had smoked a pipe constantly since leaving Virginia and he might have been the first European victim of tobacco-smoke poisoning.

Foodstuffs

Some of the crops the English knew from home grew almost wherever seeds were dropped in the new land. Wheat was grown, and barley, oats, peas, beans, melons, and gourds were plentiful. But the most important food crop was *pagatowr,* which the English call maize and Americans now call corn. The kernels came in different colors—white, yellow, red, and blue. Multicolored corn is still called "Indian corn" today. After grinding the kernels and mixing the meal with water, people made fine bread by baking *pagatowr* on flat stones. They also made a tasty porridge by boiling it. The company brewed a good ale from it. *Pagatowr* grew well, ripened quickly, and showed much promise for commerce.

The sugar cane that Harriot brought from the West Indies did not grow, and he believed that it was too late in the season for it to prosper. Since the climate seemed warm, Harriot believed that oranges and lemons would also grow in Virginia. He was wrong, as he was about other aspects of climate. He erroneously thought that all of the New World had the same climate.

Walnuts were plentiful, and walnut oil, Tom thought, was likely to be a good export. Fruits such as grapes, strawberries, mulberries, hurts (hurtleberries), crabapples, and medlars, as well as red pears which the natives called *mutaquesunnauk* were declared delicious.

Many kinds of seeds and nuts as well as wild peas were dried, parched, and ground to be used in cooking. Almost every household had a stone mortar to grind *pagatowr,* seeds, and other foodstuffs to make them easy to cook. These stones came from the distant hills and were not found on Roanoke Island.

Roots were also used for food. *Operauk* (peanuts), leeks, and others that the natives called *okeepenauk, kaishucpenauk, tsinaw, coscushaw* or *cassava* for flour, and *habascon* (cow parsnip) could be dug and ground into meal.

The Algonquians made use of most of the animals in the area as meat.

"Their sitting at meate."

Their feetheynge of their meate in XV.
earthen pottes.

"Their seetheynge of their meate in earthen pottes."

There were deer, rabbits, squirrels, bears, turkeys, partridges, doves, and in winter, Harriot was told, there would be swans and geese. Tom Harriot learned the names of twenty-eight other beasts, but he did not see more than twelve of them. There was no doubt in his mind that there were many edible animals in the forests.

The men caught fish with weirs (nets made of reeds), or with sharpened spears much like the darts that fishermen used in Ireland. Herring larger than those in English waters, sturgeon aplenty, trout, porpoises, rays, oldwives, mullets, plaice, and many other excellent fish were for the catching. Crabs, oysters, mussels, scallops, periwinkles, and lobsters also came from various parts of the waters that surrounded Roanoke Island. Sea turtles, which seemed ugly because of their thick shells, were good eating, and their eggs were also delicious.

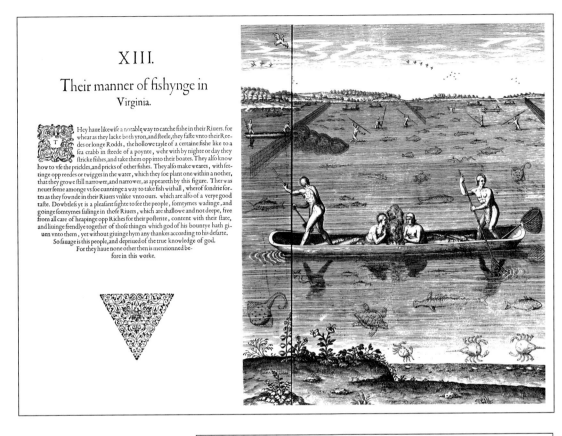

XIII.

Their manner of fishynge in Virginia.

Hey haue likewise a notable way to catche fishe in their Riuers. for wheat as they lacke both yron, and steele, they faste vnto their Reedes or longe Rodds, the hollowe tayle of a certaine fishe like to a sea crabb in steede of a poynte, wehr with by nighte or day they stricke fishes, and take them opp into their boates. They also know how to vse the prickles, and pricks of other fishes. They also make weares, with settinge opp reedes or twigges in the water, which they soe plant one within a nother, that they growe still narrower, and narrower, as appeareth by this figure. Ther was neuer seene amonge vs soe cunninge a way to take fish withall, wherof sondrie sortes as they fownde in their Riuers vnlike vnto ours. which are also of a verye good taste. Dowbtlefs yt is a pleasant sighte to see the people, somtymes wadinge, and goinge somtymes sailinge in thofe Riuers, which are shallowe and not deepe, free from all care of heapinge opp Riches for their posterite, content with their state, and liuinge frendlye together of thofe thinges which god of his bountye hath giuen vnto them, yet without giuinge hym any thankes according to his desarte.

So sauage is this people, and depriued of the true knowledge of god. For they haue none other then is mentionned before in this worke.

The brovvyllinge of their fishe   XIIII.
ouer the flame.

Above: "Their manner of fishynge in Virginia."

Right: "The brovvyllinge of their fishe ouer the flame."

Building Materials

Commodities for building houses and ships were plentiful: trees, stone, lime, and the makings of brick. Straight and tall oaks for good timber were abundant, as were large walnut trees, fir trees for ship masts, hard maple, beech, ash, elm, cedar, witch hazel, cypress, laurel, and holly, as well as many other trees.

Near the shoreline, only pebbles washed down by streams existed. But farther up country, large stones and a gray stone similar to marble could be quarried, and there was no shortage of clay and lime that the English could use for making brick. There were plentiful discarded oyster shells which could be burned to make lime as was done in England.

There was little doubt that they were in a rich land, which the inhabitants enjoyed, even if they seemed to have little that Englishmen would call rich goods.

"The manner of makinge their boates."

Trouble

When Admiral Grenville departed for England on August 25, 1585, to obtain supplies and reinforcements, Captain Ralph Lane became governor of Virginia. Lane did not have the prudent attitude that Tom Harriot had shown toward the Algonquians. Lane wanted treasure, was short-tempered, and attacked Indian villages during his travels. Lane did not take seriously Harriot's advice to him about dealing fairly with the natives. He also made appointments with high-sounding titles which meant little. For instance, he named one of the company "Colonel of the Chesapians," and others, "Master of the Light Horsemen," "Master of the Victuals," and "Keeper of the Stores."

By late September most of the company had moved the remaining supplies from the ships to Roanoke Island. Some members of the party did not like to work and lounged about the settlement. However, the captain made sure that a small fort, which they called Fort Ralegh, was built to defend against the people he feared would turn hostile. This tiny fort has been partially restored by archeologists and can be seen by visitors to Roanoke Island today.

Winter was setting in and the food supply was low. Many of the company had not thought from the beginning that they should work at farming and, as supplies dwindled, they fought among themselves and with the Indians. King Wingina had tired of Captain Lane's military ways and had organized his people for an assault on the fort on Roanoke Island. The soldiers skirmished with the Indians, who retreated.

In mid-March, Harriot and Tom Buckner were with Captain Lane exploring the Chowan and Roanoke rivers. Captain Lane, strong and short-tempered, captured a crippled Indian, Mentonon, and kept him in chains for two days while questioning him about Wingina's revolt. He released him, but sent Mentonon's favorite son, Skiko, back to Fort Ralegh in a pinnace as a hostage.

The forty soldiers in the exploring party had become weary of Lane. They were hungry and exhausted and resented the captain's hard-driving search for gold and pearls while they were reduced to eating dog stew and boiled sassafras leaves. They threatened to revolt and Lane ordered the party home. On their way back to the fort on Easter Sunday, April 3, they located Indian weirs full of fish, emptied them, and had their first full meal in days.

Wingina's braves gathered to attack the Roanoke Island settlement. Through a ruse, Captain Lane gained access to Wingina and fired on him and his supporters. Wingina was wounded and fled into the woods. He was then killed by one of Lane's men, Edward Nugent. Needless to say, this did not endear the Englishmen to the Indians.

Harriot was disappointed in the way the soldiers behaved. In a rare negative report to Ralegh he wrote about some of the party who toward the end of the year "shewed themselves too ferce in slaying some of the people."

The settlers understandably became anxious about their survival. They were ready to return home, especially since Admiral Grenville had not arrived with supplies and reinforcements as he had promised.

Since September 1585, Sir Francis Drake had been roaming the Spanish Main as a corsair, searching for ships with treasure. In Florida he learned that the Spanish were planning to attack the Roanoke colony before it could become a threat to their control of Florida. Drake sailed north to see how he could help his countrymen. Neither Lane nor Harriot knew when—or if—Grenville would arrive, and so Drake's offer to take them off the island was welcomed. Isolation, the threat of starvation, attack by the Indians, and internal distrust and strife among the colonials made the rescue offer very acceptable, even to Tom.

It became necessary for them to leave Roanoke Island hastily on June 18, 1586. A heavy four-day storm of the kind called a hurricane in the West Indies, had kept Sir Francis's ship from approaching land, and he had to put out to sea before he could anchor. Drake picked up the settlers only after the hurricane subsided. Unfortunately, three settlers who were inland on a mission had to be left behind and were never heard from again.

Harriot reported to Ralegh when he returned to England, and his printed report proved to be very important to the development of the New World. There had been other reports by travelers, but none was as thorough and detailed as Tom's. His statements and descriptions made many comparisons with old world plants and creatures. Overall, his tale was believable and his new discoveries rang true. Some of the other explorers had spun unbelievable tales.

The table of contents to Tom's final report of 1590 (the deBry edition) is reproduced on the next page as a summary of his findings. You can see that it included English and Algonquian terms. When you read it, remember that v and w were represented by u, and that ss looked something like f. The spelling of some words is different from modern spelling, too.

A TABLE
OF THE PRINCI-
PALL THINGES THAT
are contained in this Hiftorie, after the
order of the Alphabet.

A.		E.	
Allum	7	Elme.	23
Applecrabs	17	F.	
Ashe	23	Faulcons	19
Afcopo.	23	Flaxe and Hempe	7
B.		Fiere trees	23
Beares	17	Furres	9
Beech.	23	G.	
C.		Geefe	19
Cedar	9.23	Crappes	17
Cheftnuts	17	H.	
Ciuet Cattes	9	Habafcon	15
Conies	19	Hau they bwild their houfes	24
Cofcuhaw	15	Haukes	19
Copper	9	Hernes	19
Cranes	19	Herrings	19
Creuifes	21	Holly	23
D.		Hurleberies.	17
Deare	19	I.	
Deare skinnes	9	Iron.	9
Dyes of diuers kindes.	11	K.	
		*K*aishucpenauk	15

F   3

"A Table of the Principall Things that are contained in this Historie, after the order of the Alphabet."

The Table.

Harriot's Table *from Kewafowok . . .*

The Table.

F   I   N   I   S.

. . . *to Worme Silke.*

CHAPTER 7

Home Again

THESE OTHER THINGS WERE HAPPENING
> 1587 · *Hideyoshi banned Portuguese missionaries from Japan.*
> 1587 · *John Winthrop became the first governor of the Massachusetts Bay Colony.*
> 1589 · *King Henry of Navarre renounced Protestantism and became King Henry IV of France, saying, "Paris is worth a Mass."*
> 1589 · *Forks were used for the first time in the French Court.*

During the survey of Virginia, the explorers were out of touch with England except for rare news from a visiting ship. Much was going on in Europe. While the explorers were far from home, Ralegh was active in Queen Elizabeth's court.

Ralegh seemed to be in constant motion. He worked hard for success, and expected the same of others. The queen was equally demanding in a more regal way, and Ralegh's intellectual and social skills were taxed to keep up with her and other members of her council, most of whom were his competitors. He was a good advisor and his ideas were accepted by the capricious queen most of the time.

Sir Walter was a stimulating person who could write poetry for the queen, could anticipate her every wish, and could attend to her whims. It was hard work, but it paid Ralegh well. Harriot was kept busy by his patron's expectations and demands when he returned home.

The Spanish government, worried about the inroads the English were making in Florida and the West Indies, built new ships and prepared for an invasion of England. They hoped to reestablish the Roman Catholic Church as well as control the English privateers who were capturing their treasure-laden ships on the way home from South America. The Spanish threat was a serious one. The English were worried and prepared for an invasion.

After they returned from Roanoke, Tom and John White were well received by Walter Ralegh at Youghal in Ireland. Ralegh encouraged Harriot to write a report for publication quickly so that he could further promote English colonies in the New World. In addition, he asked Tom to help build up his Irish estates. The farms and houses were in poor condition, for most of Ireland had been made destitute by war and famine. Tom sailed back and forth between London and Youghal, taking care of Sir Walter's financial affairs.

Ralegh had done very well financially. The queen was unusually generous with her favorite. She made him Captain of the Guard and provided him with fruitful monopolies. He was made warden of the Stannaries, and therefore controlled the tin production in Cornwall. He was made rich by a wine monopoly. Every cask of wine sold in England and every tavern license granted swelled his fortune. Harriot had the great responsibility of trying to keep up with Ralegh's complicated finances.

After the great adventure in the New World both Tom Harriot and Tom Buckner were well known in London. Buckner opened his own mercer's shop on Threadneedle Street, which was visited by customers who wanted to hear about Virginia and its riches. He never tired of entertaining them while showing bolts of cloth. After Sir Walter Ralegh sent his own tailor to him for material, he gained even more business. Buckner married a woman from Oxfordshire, and became a solid citizen and a vestryman in St. Christopher's parish church.

Tom Harriot remained a mathematician, and Ralegh continued his support of Harriot's inquiring mind. In the preface to a publication dedicated to Ralegh, the well-known geographer Richard Hakluyt praised Ralegh for his interest in mathematical navigation and for "having maintained in your household

Thomas Hariot, a man preeminent in those studies, at a most liberal salary." Tom was firmly in Ralegh's favor.

Tom was given his own estate. Ralegh granted him the Abbey of Molanna on the island of Dair-inis in the Blackwater River north of Youghal. This ancient abbey was founded in 501 A.D. by Saint Mael-Anfaidh. It was in constant religious use for a thousand years until 1585, when it was transferred, as a part of the English Reformation, from the bishopric of Lismore to its first lay owner, Sir Walter Ralegh. John White also received an estate nearby, and the two men continued to survey and map Ralegh holdings as well as their own.

While Tom was in Ireland mapping Ralegh's Lismore estate he followed up his work on the Algonquian language by developing new ways to represent speech sounds by symbols.

John White returned to Roanoke as the head of another group of settlers, including his own family. His daughter Elinor married one of the settlers, Ananias Dare, and bore a daughter, who was the first child of English origin born in the colonies, Virginia Dare. After White returned to England, the colony vanished and thereafter was called "The Lost Colony." A popular outdoor drama of that name is performed every summer at the Waterside Theater at Manteo on Roanoke Island, now in the State of North Carolina. It tells the story of the possible fate of this tragic group. Near the entrance to the outdoor theater is a woodland trail called the Thomas Harriot Nature Walk. Visitors can see most of the trees and shrubs that Harriot listed in his report. The restored Fort Ralegh is nearby.

Correspondence with Mathematicians

Tom exchanged mathematical ideas with colleagues in England and on the Continent. His easy use of Latin paid off when he corresponded with German, Italian, or French mathematicians. He was accepted by them as a leader in navigational science and theoretical mathematics, and his contributions were referred to in works of both practical and advanced mathematical theory. London's booksellers knew Tom as a good customer, for he was forever ordering books he had learned about from his many friends. He could afford to buy almost any book he needed.

The mathematician and mapmaker John Dee had been convinced that there was a Northwest Passage near latitude 37 degrees (in the vicinity of the Roanoke colony) which connected the Atlantic and Pacific oceans. A map he had drawn for Sir Humphrey Gilbert in 1582 showed such a passage. Although he could not believe in Dee's theoretical "passage," Harriot was very pleased when John Dee inscribed one of his books, "Ex Dono Thomae Hariot, Amicae Mei [my friend]."

John Dee

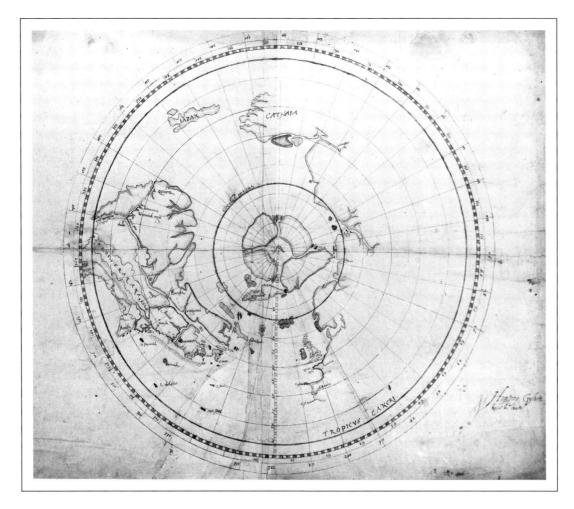

Dee's possible Northwest Passage

English Interest in Shipbuilding and Ordnance

In 1586 most Englishmen were concerned about preparing for war with Spain. English spies reported a great buildup of Spanish ships, and both sides believed that war was inevitable.

Harriot had long been interested in building efficient ships, and had disagreed with the queen's master shipwright, Mathew Baker, on their design. He criticized Baker by first quoting him: "It is knowne by experience that a ship whose depth is .10 foote, breadth, .20 and length is .50 by the keel is of burden 100 tone." He questioned Baker's ratio on several grounds. Better, said Harriot, to obtain the bulk of a ship by determining the volume of its displacement. He examined many ships, measured some, and recorded the measurements made by others when he knew he could depend upon them.

Tom became very much involved with ordnance, for he and the English leaders had never been satisfied with the prowess of naval gunners. Accurate cannon fire can make a great difference in a naval engagement, for when a mast and its rigging are hit solidly, the ship is often disabled and made useless.

In 1587 Harriot obtained a copy of William Bourne's book, *The Arte of Shooting with Great Ordinance*. Bourne challenged the Aristotelian doctrine of motion, and Tom believed that it should be challenged if the English were ever to learn to hit their targets. Experienced cannoneers believed that the only guaranteed way to hit a naval target was to come alongside and shoot at point-blank range.

The Spanish Armada

The Spanish massed a giant fleet to conquer Protestant England, and there was much defensive activity on the part of the English. In Devon, great stories of the coming Spanish invasion were on everyone's lips. As a part of the war effort Sir Walter Ralegh went to the West Country to recruit men from the Stannaries to reinforce the coastal defenses of Cornwall and the island of Portland, of which he was governor. When Ralegh was named warden of the Stannaries he became very popular with the tin miners because he stabilized metal prices, organized the mines successfully, and made the miners more prosperous. Ralegh had very little difficulty raising the men he needed to defend their homes.

The actual naval action began in July 1588. The first sea battle was in its third day when Ralegh joined the fleet. He hoped that the lighter English ships could outmaneuver the great Spanish galleons and that the usual hard summer storms off the English coast would confuse the Spanish. Tom Harriot did not fight actively, but continued to gather information, assemble maps and charts, as well as serve as overseer of the Ralegh holdings and estates while his patron was otherwise engaged. Eventually the Spanish Armada was driven off and escaped, badly beaten, by sailing north past Scotland and then to Ireland and Spain. The Spanish had little food and almost no fresh water, and the sailors suffered badly. In Ireland, where they landed in hopes of getting fresh water, they were attacked by the inhabitants and driven off.

Cannonballs

In preparation for the Spanish invasion, Ralegh had asked Tom, "What is the best way to stack cannonballs?" He needed to know how much floor space was needed to store heavy iron balls on a ship or at a fort. Cannonballs, being round, are a nuisance in the hold or on the deck of a ship. But gunners need to know how many cannonballs are available for use and exactly where they are.

Tom solved the problem of stacking them efficiently through mathematics. Without picking up any cannonballs, except to measure a few, he provided Ralegh with a quick reference chart so that it was possible to read directly the number of cannonballs on the ground or on a pyramidal pile with a triangular, square, or rectangular base. Harriot worked this out entirely by using mathematical laws of progression.

As he often did, Tom moved from the practical to the theoretical and back. He graphed all the possible configurations that separate particles might assume and made charts to illustrate his calculations, so that a gunner could tell how many shots he had left. Since one of the problems that both the English and Spanish captains had during this battle, the first modern naval campaign, was to accurately supply powder and shot for their cannons, Tom's contribution was important for the English victory.

Tom also thought that by showing the many configurations that discrete particles can assume, his calculations could lead to demonstrating the atomic theory of matter, which was not yet accepted by all Elizabethan scientists.

When Tom was experimenting with the rate of fall of musket balls from the windows of his room in Durham House, he couldn't get his calculations to work. After a while, he realized that the blunder he had made was in accepting Aristotle's concept that heavy bodies fall at a faster rate than do light bodies. Until he realized Aristotle's error he was disappointed with his measurements.

He recovered when he realized that heavy and light bodies fall at the same rate, as Galileo Galilei had found. This experience strengthened his belief that old ways of thinking need to be doubted and reexamined constantly.

Harriot's New World Report

Harriot's interim report on the New World was finally published in 1588. It was in folio edition, printed on cheap paper, and sold for a few pennies. He gave copies to his close friends, including Tom Buckner. The forty-eight-page pamphlet included a brief preface by Governor Ralph Lane to attest to its accuracy. Naturally, it was dedicated to Sir Walter Ralegh. Only six copies have survived to the present day.

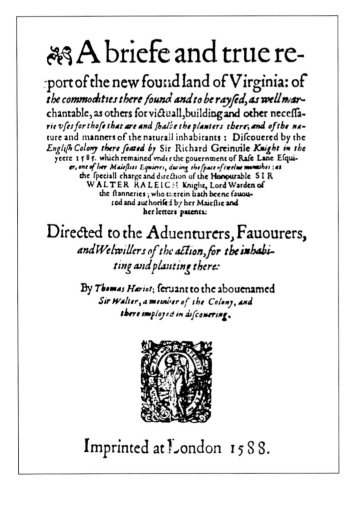

Title page, 1588 Edition of
A Briefe and True Report of the New Founde Land of Virginia

Interest in Tom's pamphlet was much greater after Richard Hakluyt praised it. Hakluyt reprinted it in the next edition of his *Principal Navigations*. He also recommended its translation into Latin, French, and German to Theodore deBry who became interested in publishing it together with some of John White's illustrations.

Although Harriot did not consider himself a specialist in the future sciences of anthropology, botany, horticulture, geology, chemistry, metallurgy, linguistics,

Title page, 1590 De Bry Edition of A Briefe and True Report of the New Founde Land of Virginia

or zoology, his experiences in Virginia showed that he had considerable knowledge in these areas and had brought forth new discoveries in those fields.

Since Harriot never published his other findings throughout his life, it is tempting to wonder whether Sir Walter, with his great concern for influencing the queen to support additional voyages of exploration, prodded Tom to prepare his notes for publication every time he saw him. It is also tempting to wonder whether Ralegh's constant nagging—and the labors involved in writing for the printer, reading proofs, and answering the many questions involved in producing even small brochures—did not color Tom's attitude toward publishing his scientific findings later in his life. We know that he prepared reports for his patrons when he needed to, for his rough drafts have survived, but actual publication requires time and labor that he might not have wanted to expend.

The interim publication's impact was immediate, and two years later the illustrated publication, *A Briefe and True Report of the New Found Land of Virginia* was issued in English, French, German, and Latin editions, in the large folio size common at the time. Twenty-eight of White's original watercolors were engraved by Theodore deBry, and deBry added additional engravings.

Reproductions of the original deBry edition are still available. Dover Publications of New York issued an excellent reproduction in 1972 from a copy that Lessing J. Rosenwald presented to the Library of Congress. The reprinted book is also available in Canada and Great Britain.

Trouble Brewing

Sir Walter secretly married Elizabeth Throckmorton, the queen's lady-in-waiting, in 1587. This foreshadowed trouble for both of them. The queen did not like to be kept in the dark, nor did she want her ladies-in-waiting to marry without her consent. For a time the queen did not react, keeping the couple on tenterhooks.

Ralegh searched for a suitable estate for his new family and thought that he had found one, Sherbourne Castle in Dorset. He petitioned the queen to transfer it from Bishop Caldwell and grant it to him, but he did not hear from her for some time. She seemed less willing to please him.

Northumberland

Sir Walter and young Henry Percy, the ninth earl of Northumberland, had become very friendly. Like many gentlemen they both enjoyed gambling. They enjoyed each other's company and liked to do the same things. Sometimes they even dressed alike and their horses' saddles were identically straw colored.

*Henry Percy,
the Ninth Earl of
Northumberland*

After having supper with the earl of Northumberland and Sir Walter, Harriot confided to Tom Buckner that he was excited about dining in such exalted company. One of the other guests was Henry Wriothesley, the third earl of Southampton, the patron of the poet and playwright William Shakespeare, who dedicated his sonnets to him as W. H.

Apparently Northumberland was somewhat deaf and found conversation with strangers difficult. The queen had asked him to be ambassador to France, but he made the excuse that he might misunderstand what was being said and this could embarrass the queen and all England. She accepted this excuse.

When Tom was analyzing speech sounds and symbols to represent the Algonquian language in Virginia he did not know that he was honing his ability to discriminate among speech sounds and that this would be socially fruitful. As a result of his analysis he learned how to speak clearly to Northumberland so that the earl could easily understand him.

Harriot became a regular diner at the earl's table. In the breving-book in which the earl's guests were recorded, he was listed as having dined there fifty-one times from September 21, 1591 through the next seventy-four days! Northumberland liked Tom. Not only could he understand him easily when he spoke, but the Earl respected his curious mind, mathematical ability, and his willingness to explore ideas.

Northumberland, Tom said to Tom Buckner, spoke thoughtfully and was a prudent, temperate man, even though he had great wealth and power. Tom was interested in more security than Ralegh's patronage could give him and looked toward the earl of Northumberland as a possible source of support.

CHAPTER 8

New Support

THESE OTHER THINGS WERE HAPPENING

1591 · *James Lancaster left Plymouth for the first English voyage to the East Indies.*

1592 · *William Shakespeare was mentioned as an actor for the first time. His plays* Richard III *and* Comedy of Errors *were performed in London.*

1592 · *Windmills were first used in Holland to drive mechanical saws.*

1595 · *Heels first appeared on shoes.*

Thomas Harriot always remembered that Walter Ralegh had helped him get a good start in life after his graduation from Oxford. The active Ralegh, too, always remained loyal to his aide, Harriot. Ralegh continued to provide Harriot with living quarters at Durham House, Devon, Dorset, and Ireland.

In 1592, soon after the birth of Ralegh's son, "Wat," the queen actively showed her displeasure with her former favorite. Ralegh and his family were imprisoned in the Tower of London. Harriot continued his important financial duties and remained a friend even when the Raleghs were in prison.

The Madre de Deus

It was ironic that the queen, very soon after casting the Ralegh family into the Tower, decided to free Ralegh to save herself from financial loss. The richest prize ship English privateers had captured in her reign, the *Madre de Deus*, was taken by Ralegh's own ship, the *Roebuck*. "The Great Carrack," as the prize ship was nicknamed in England, was taken to Dartmouth harbor about a month after the Raleghs were imprisoned. Rumors of its fabulous wealth spread, and swindlers came from all over the country to buy or steal the cargo. Even the *Roebuck* sailors helped with the pillaging.

The queen's advisors told her that only the popular Sir Walter could control the situation, and so she sent him, with a keeper, Sir Christopher Blount, to protect the treasure. Within a half hour of his arrival, Ralegh had stopped the looting and retrieved much of the stolen property. For this he was given his family's freedom, although he remained in the queen's disfavor.

As soon as Harriot received word of the great ship's arrival, he sailed to Dartmouth to obtain detailed measurements of the *Madre de Deus*, for it was of an unusual design which might serve to improve English ships. Harriot continued his interest in shipbuilding until Ralegh's death in 1618. When his patron no longer would profit from his knowledge of ships, Tom's interest turned to other subjects.

In 1593, Harriot was still mapping Ralegh's Irish estates. Perhaps the plague that was ravaging London at the time encouraged him to keep a safe distance from the big city.

Good News

June 26, 1593, on the occasion of his being installed into the Most Noble Order of the Garter at Windsor Castle, Henry Percy, the ninth earl of Northumberland gave a gift of £80 to Harriot. This was the start of an annual patronage grant to Master "heriat," as his name was written in the earl's official records. The amount of the gift was a significant one, for the chief officers of the Earl's household were paid only £10 to £20 for a full year's service. Tom Harriot was doing well.

Suspicion of Atheism

The popular hysteria of the time about a mathematician's atheism still hovered over Harriot, and Ralegh's high position had gained him enemies. A Jesuit named Robert Parsons attacked "Sir Walter Ralegh's School of Atheism and the conjuror [Harriot] who is master thereof," fueling the zeal of orthodox Anglicans to root out atheists and other religious dissenters. Parsons also attacked others in Queen Elizabeth's court. Father Parsons's treatise was in answer to the queen's proclamation of October 18, 1591, which attacked the seminary priests and Jesuits who were working secretly to convert the English to Catholicism. It was not the first charge of atheism leveled at Harriot. At a trial of poet Christopher Marlowe, Richard Baines was recorded as saying, "Moyses was but a Jugler, (magician) and that one Heriots being Sir Walter Ralegh's man can do more than he."

To investigate the charges against Ralegh and Harriot, an ecclesiastical commission was held in Cerne Abbas in March 1594. No guilt was assigned to the accused, but Harriot became even more mysterious to the gossiping public.

Sir Walter's public reputation did not suffer, and soon after the Cerne Abbas commission was concluded, the indefatigable Ralegh started to collect money for an expedition to Guiana. Harriot, as always, kept the accounts. But he was now more independent as the result of Henry Percy's support.

Northumberland's Further Generosity

As a companion of the ninth earl, Tom Harriot often played cards with him in the evening. The earl's record of the time shows that on June 11, 1596 the earl lost 12 pence at "faysh," which was based on the drawing of cards. One wonders whether the modern game of "go fish" is similar to, or descended from "faysh."

Northumberland's residence, Syon House, was on the River Thames in Isleworth Hundred just across from Kew Gardens. It was just three hours from London by boat—the fastest way to commute—and far enough away for privacy but close enough for ready access to the court if necessary.

Northumberland offered Harriot a house of his own as a residence and laboratory only a hundred yards from the main house. It was perfect for Tom's needs, quiet enough for working and close enough to London for Ralegh-related business. Although Syon House is still standing, Harriot's dwelling has long been destroyed.

Tom started working with lenses at Syon, and the growing field of optics required clear night skies if he was to observe the stars. At Syon he could work all night if he wished. A list of the housewarming gifts given him by the earl when he took over the Syon residence in 1597 included, according to the earl's records, "dyverse pewther vessels and Pottes."

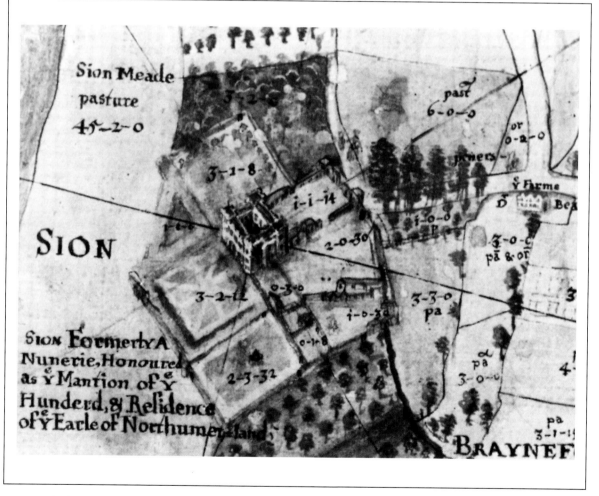

General plan, Syon

Brampton

In addition, the generous earl gave Harriot the rights to a handsome property in Brampton (sometimes called Barmaton) in the Bishopric of Durham, to the north. This made Harriot a member of the landed gentry and assured him an independent income from rents. The indenture provided that Harriot pay £4 per year to the earl of Northumberland for this privilege, a relatively small amount.

With the Brampton property and his pension, Tom Harriot was comfortable at Syon and able to maintain his own staff of servants. He was well off, thanks to the earl, and could continue his scientific work. Ralegh was no longer his only support.

No one knows how many problems Thomas Harriot solved during his lifetime. He seemed to work best when he was challenged by a question that interested him. His working sheets—over eight thousand of them are known—are undated for the most part. Many of them are fragments. They are stored in various places. Most of them, Harrioteers believe, are in the British Library, in Petworth House in Sussex, and in Alnwick Castle, where the Syon records were moved. But none were actually printed and published in Harriot's time, except, of course, the *Briefe and True Report.*

When we examine his lifework, it must be an incomplete review. He did not make it easy to locate and organize his contributions. Although his work was almost always related to mathematics, he moved from theoretical computation to navigation to optics to astronomy to chemistry or physics, depending upon how he was stimulated to work. At one time he wrote a friend that he would "rather doe something worth nothinge than nothinge at all." He simply *had* to keep busy.

We cannot organize his work into subject matter year by year without oversimplifying his motivation, his interests, and his mental processes. His output was occasionally curtailed by outside influences, such as when Ralegh was on trial, but even when his friends Ralegh or Northumberland were confined in the Tower of London, Tom worked constantly, except for an occasional visit to the Tower to see them. When Harriot's health first started to weaken at the age of forty-five he apparently lost little of his curiosity and drive to learn. He was still active and did much scientific work. Although Thomas Harriot was an orderly, systematic worker (except for not dating the pages of his work), his records did not remain orderly after his death. In the next three chapters some of his important projects are discussed. Although they follow his life span, they are not necessarily in calendar order.

We know that Tom was friendly with other writers and poets, such as Christopher Marlowe. There is no direct evidence that he ever met William Shakespeare. It is possible, however, that they had some contacts. We must remember that a complete and educated Elizabethan gentleman was expected to write well and to be able to use language appropriately.

The great poet Edmund Spenser was one of Ralegh's close friends when they both lived in Ireland. Other poets, such as George Peel and Matthew Royden, were students at Oxford when Tom was enrolled in St. Mary's Hall. Another fellow Oxonian, George Chapman, included in the first section of *Achilles Shield* a portrayal of Harriot:

> *To you whose depth of soule measures the height,*
> *And all dimensions of all workes of weight,*
> *Reason being ground, structure and ornament,*
> *To all inventions, grave and permanent,*
> *And your cleare eyes the Spheres where Reason moves . . .*

Harriot's interests ranged wide, and he had many friends.

Original Discoveries?

Even today, individual scientists rarely discover or invent things completely independently. A number of scientists may have the same idea at almost the same time. Sometimes they borrow from one another or develop insights from someone else's work. Thomas Harriot was a part of the scientific community of his day, and whether he was the first to make a discovery is something we cannot always show. Others worked on the same problems. There is no doubt, however, that Harriot was one of the scientific pioneers of his time.

CHAPTER 9

Mathematics, Ciphers, and Codes

THESE OTHER THINGS WERE HAPPENING

1604 · *Peace existed between England and Spain.*

1611 · *Authorized version of the Bible—the King James Bible—published in England.*

1612 · *The Dutch used Manhattan Island as a fur-trading center for the first time.*

1613 · *Fire destroyed the Globe Theater, in which Shakespeare's plays were performed.*

1615 · *Galileo faced the Inquisition for the first time.*

A modern mathematician, Jon Pepper, has called Tom Harriot "The most symbolically original and fluent algebraist of his time." Unfortunately, Harriot left no explanations or calculations in his notes, leaving it to the reader to supply the mathematical justification for his algebraic ideas. This places a considerable burden on the reader, who must enter Harriot's thinking processes—no mean feat.

Although geometry and algebra developed as separate subjects, mathematicians such as Harriot found it easy to describe geometric shapes by algebraic equations. One well-known equation that illustrates this is $C^2 = A^2 + B^2$, the Pythagorean theorem. It is used to calculate the hypotenuse of a right-angled triangle. Expressing geometric ideas in algebraic symbols was not a Western invention. A Chinese book of the third century A.D. used algebraic equations to describe geometrical figures and to express geometrical propositions. In 825 A.D. an Arab, Al-Khowarizmi, published a book, *Hisab al-jabr wal muqabalah* which explained how to solve quadratic equations. "Al-jabr" became algebra, and Al-Khowarizmi was corrupted to "algorithm."

Algebra and the Theory of Equations

The beginnings of algebra in Europe are complex, and date from the thirteenth century when Leonardo Pisano adapted Hindu-Arabic numeration. From then on, algebra's history was clouded with national pride. English, French, Italian, Austrian, and German mathematicians joined in a series of controversies over who discovered what that lasted over centuries. Harriot's work was done in the midst of this furor.

He based his system on the work of the ancients and the Frenchman François Vieta. A nineteenth-century Harrioteer, Henry Stevens, wrote, "His modifications, improvements, and simplifications were so distinct that from the first, and long before publication, they were called among his students and correspondents as Harriot's Method."

He introduced elementary algebra much as it is today as far as notation and some results are concerned. The idea of placing terms on one side of the equality sign and then factorizing from that point appeared first in Harriot's *Artis Analyticae Praxis.* Even the inequality signs < for "is less than" and > for "is greater than" were first used by Harriot.

René Descartes (1596–1650), the great French philosopher, has sometimes been credited with inventing algebra. After his death an English partisan accused him of borrowing his basic algebraic doctrine from Harriot. Only after Harrioteers, searching through his mass of papers, proved that Harriot had credited Vieta's contributions and that Harriot had done his mathematical work in 1596, when Descartes was an infant, did the idea that Descartes had originated algebra subside. There is no doubt that Harriot enriched algebra with a comprehensive theory of equations and many other important contributions.

About two hundred years later, in 1814, William Spense wrote *Outlines of a Theory of Algebraical Equations deduced from the Principles of Harriott and extended to Fluxional or differential Calculus.* In the preface he said, "Until the publication of Harriot's *Artis Analyticae Praxis*, no theory of equations was given. Harriot considered algebraic equations merely as analytic expressions, detached wholly from the operations by which they might be individually produced; and, carrying all the terms over to one side, he assumed the hypothesis that, as in that state the equation was equal to nothing, it could always be reduced to as many simple factors as there were units in the index of its highest power." It was six years after his death that Harriot's system of algebra became familiar to more than his close friends and students, who had known about his work for thirty years.

In his will, Harriot left specific instructions for the publication of his algebra text, *Artis Analyticae Praxis*, even describing the location of his manuscript. He appointed an old Oxford friend, Nathaniel Torporley, as his literary executor. However, work on the manuscript was delayed for six years, even though the earl of Northumberland pressed for its publication and subsidized the edition. It is possible that Torporley did not agree with some of the ideas in the manuscript, or that he did not fully understand them, or both. Walter Warner later became the editor, possibly with the help of Thomas Aylesbury.

According to many knowledgeable mathematicians, the result was a poor representation of Harriot's thinking. However, an examination of Harriot's papers makes it understandable that a lesser mathematician than Harriot would likely be confused by the mass of material he left. Many hundreds of pages had only calculations, and no words whatever. The reader must construct the mathematical thinking with little help from Harriot.

Navigation and Solid Geometry

Harriot had learned early in his career that navigation on the sea involved spherical geometry. He had studied the most recent book on the subject, Holywood's *Sphaera Mundi*, before his journeys to the New World. But he continued his interest in solid geometry far beyond the Virginia voyages with studies of rhumb lines and the interpretation of the relatively new Mercator map. Rhumb lines can be described as the separate lines made with a knife on an orange when the rind is cut top to bottom. The Mercator map, a means of depicting a globe on a flat surface, is familiar to us, but it was new to most Elizabethans.

Sections of Cones

Conic sections revealed the innermost secrets of basic forms such as ellipses, parabolas, and hyperbolas. These forms were not a part of the old Euclidean geometry.

Their mathematical analysis led to exciting discoveries about the behavior of natural phenomena. The earth's path around the sun or the path of a projectile through the air could be expressed mathematically through algebraic equations. Harriot was at the forefront of this development.

The Area of Spherical Triangles

On September 18, 1603, Harriot explained in his notes how to compute the area of a spherical triangle: "Take the sum of all three angles and subtract 180 degrees. Set the remainder as numerator of a fraction with the denominator 360 degrees. This fraction tells how great a portion of the hemisphere is occupied by the triangle." This was one of Harriot's few precisely dated and simply explained computations.

In about 1614 he returned to his study of rhumb lines and the interpretation of the Mercator map. He nearly finished a table of meridional parts for the map, with computations calculated for one-minute intervals. For interpolating finite differences, Harriot wrote a treatise (unpublished, to be sure), *De numeris triangulais.*

Harriot understood that when negative integers or fractions are used as n, they are operational. Other Europeans were suspicious of negative numbers, for they were considered "imaginaries" or "impossibles." The Chinese, however, had used them on the abacus as early as the second century B.C. They were represented by black rods, while positive numbers were represented by red rods on the abacus. The law of sines was in full use by 1299 A.D. in China, but was only partially stated in Europe about four hundred years later.

Ciphers, Codes, and Suspicion

Queen Elizabeth died in March 1603 and James IV of Scotland ascended the English throne as King James I of England. In the same year, the plague once again struck London. In the midst of this tumult, Tom was working on ciphers and codes. He played with letters and numbers, taking pleasure in the secrets he could hide from others who did not know the proper code. This fascination with secrecy probably added to his reputation as a necromancer.

The new king was a very suspicious man. One of his advisors, Sir Robert Cecil, soon influenced him to remove Walter Ralegh as a favorite of the court. Ralegh was accused of plotting against the king and by mid-July was again in the Tower of London. Since Tom was a known friend and accomplice of Ralegh, he too was under suspicion, but he was not jailed. However, he temporarily ceased work on most of his projects.

At this time he decided to take stock of his professional reputation. He jotted down twenty-seven books published between 1587 and 1602 in which reference was made to him and his work. We can only hope that completing this list made him feel better, for the imprisonment of his friend Ralegh was a severe blow to him.

Binary Numbers

Tom's far-ranging mathematical mind experimented with number systems and reduced traditional decimal numbers into combinations of zeros and ones—a binary system. These are some of the equivalents:

DECIMAL	BINARY	DECIMAL	BINARY
0	0	10	1010
1	1	11	1011
2	10	12	1100
3	11	13	1101
4	100	14	1110
5	101	15	1111
6	110	16	10000
7	111	17	10001
8	1000	32	100000
9	1001		

Tom thought that the binary system of numeration might make computing simpler, but he wondered how it could be put into common use. He could not foresee the electronic computer, which is based upon the split-second electronic use of binary numeration.

Mathematical Puzzles

Tom was invited to teach two students of great note—Sir John Harington and Harington's close friend Henry, Prince of Wales. Harriot loaned books to Sir John (which he was likely to do only for his most trusted friends) and the three worked on mathematical puzzles such as magic squares, a sort of acrostic. Magic squares are composed of cells that are given numerical values which, when added together vertically, horizontally, or diagonally, result in the same sum. One such magic square, which was labeled *Henricus Princeps Fecit*, produced 739,024 combinations of those three words. The phrase *Silo Princeps Fecit* was worked on one 17 by 17 square to produce 51,480 combinations. Was Tom helping the prince work with ciphers for his possible future use as king? His connection with the prince was fortunate for Tom, for it gave him personal contact with King James I.

Playing Cards

Tom was an excellent card player. He sensed when his opponents held winning cards and he calculated the mathematical odds almost unconsciously. Only the best gamblers dared to challenge him. Sir Walter Ralegh was one who dared to play cards with him. Although he did not have the same formidable mathematical skills, he had audacity and was able to bluff his way through a game of cards as well as he did through palace intrigue.

The Three Magi

The ninth earl of Northumberland, Henry Percy, recognized Tom's mathematical genius. He gave him no projects or assignments directly, but respected his abilities and liked to have him around him. All he asked was that Tom pursue inquiries. He was a patron of the arts and enjoyed the company of gifted men. He also liked to play cards with him.

There was much talk about "The Wizard Earl and His Three Magi," but Tom told Tom Buckner that this was just somebody's invention. Tom's Oxford friends Robert Hues and Walter Warner often visited Percy when he was in the Tower, Harriot, Hues, Warner, and the earl discussed only matters of common interest. They never conducted experiments or used magic there. They were, however, unified in their rejection of Artistotelian ideas and acceptance of Copernican theories. All were leaders in the New Thinking.

CHAPTER 10

Optics and Astronomy

THESE OTHER THINGS WERE HAPPENING

> 1607 · *The first permanent English settlement in the New World was established in Jamestown.*
>
> 1609 · *Henry Hudson explored the Delaware Bay and Hudson River.*
>
> 1609 · *Tea of China was shipped to Europe for the first time by the Dutch East India Company.*

Optics

In Virginia Tom had awed the Algonquians by using a glass lens to set fire to dried grass. They considered it sorcery, and in a way it was a magic show. But Harriot was more interested in the cause of the heat in the converging light rays than in the theatrics.

Others in Europe were also interested in optics. In Holland, Austria, Italy, and France as well as in England investigators explored how light behaved when it traveled. Their studies were not new. In the second century B.C. in Alexandria, Egypt, when it was a center of learning, Ptolemy had published his observations. At about the same time another Egyptian, Hero of Alexandria, discovered how light was reflected at a plane surface, or how mirrors work.

Over the years, Erasmus Vitellio had written ten books on optics derived from Ptolemy. Tom had a copy of the 1572 edition of these books, published in Basel, Switzerland. It contained the best information available, but its errors were detected by Tom and other careful observers. Just because it had been published in a book was no reason to believe every word and table of refractions.

Christopher (Kit) Tooke was a lens grinder by trade who made eye glasses for people who could not see well without help. Kit was an expert workman, and he had just the special skills Harriot needed to grind lenses for his optical experiments. They worked together for over twenty years on optical matters. Kit also assisted Tom in other scientific work, often helping to make astronomical observations.

Interested in so many things, Tom had used lenses for viewing the stars with his *perspective trunckes* (telescopes) and this had started his interest in how lenses worked.

Refraction

Harriot noticed that a straight line behind a tumbler filled with water is not continuous; instead the line is displaced. What causes this shift, he asked himself. Why is the line not continuous? Tom recorded measurements of light as it went through many substances, including water, crystal spheres, tur-

Image of a horizontal bar seen through a water glass

pentine, salt water, and "spirits of wine" (alcohol). His experiments on the behavior of light resulted in very accurate tables of refracted light.

The Law of Sines

Tom was good at applying abstract ideas to common problems. His discovery of the law of sines is a good example of how he applied his mathematical skills to the way light seems to bend as it travels through transparent substances.

In trigonometry, the sine of an angle is the ratio of the side of a right-angled triangle opposite the given angle to the hypotenuse. In the diagram below, the ratio of BD to CB is the sine of the angle ACB for whatever scale the figure is drawn.

The angles at which light enters and leaves a plane surface have specific names: The angle at which a ray of light *strikes* the surface is the angle of incidence. The angle at which the light *leaves* the surface is angle of refraction. Tom recorded the ratio between the sines of the angle of incidence and the angle of refraction of many substances, and found that they were always the same for each individual substance.

Tom had discovered a major law of refraction. This is the Law of Sines of Refraction. The law was also worked out by Willebrord Snell in Holland a few decades later. Since Snell published it and Tom only made a note about it, it has been known ever since as Snell's Law of Refraction.

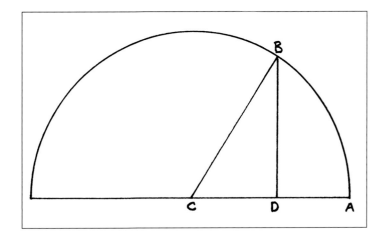

Circle showing Sine. BD, sine of arc AB; ratio of BD to CB, sine of angle ACB

Rainbows

Tom circulated his findings and conclusions about his law of refraction among some of his scientific friends. The news was carried by them to far-off Prague, where Johannes Kepler was studying the same phenomenon. Kepler wrote Tom a letter on October 2, 1606, asking him to share some of his findings on the causes of rainbows, the origins and essential differences between colors, and the halos surrounding the sun. But Tom seemed reluctant to respond. If he had followed up with a prompt response, his fame might have been assured.

Instead he wrote Kepler a brief letter two months later, pleading poor health. Maybe he was not well, or perhaps he didn't want to share his results with a stranger. Perhaps he was planning to publish them himself. He was vague in mentioning his theories of refraction, and did not mention calculation by the law of sines. He shared with Kepler a table of refraction for only ten liquids and five transparent solids, giving in each case the specific gravity and the angle of refraction in air for an incident ray of thirty degrees.

Concerning rainbows, Tom told Kepler that he expected to write on the subject if God would grant him leisure and health. He mentioned that the cause of the rainbow lay in the action of light passing through a spherical drop of water, with reflection on the concave surfaces and refraction on the convex surfaces of each drop.

In his next letter, Kepler asked Tom to define his angles of refraction and incidence. He apparently could not follow Tom's vague arguments. They wrote back and forth several times, but no warm and productive relationship resulted.

Tom observed many rainbows and studied the spectrum of colors of the rainbow, but he was never satisfied with his results. He erroneously thought that the red rays were refracted more than the blue rays. However, he finally measured the radius of the rainbow with his astronomical and navigational tools after theorizing correctly how the radius could be calculated. Again, he never published his findings but kept only a massive collection of notes.

Halley's Comet

In 1607, all of England saw the great comet which was later called Halley's Comet. Tom used two cross staffs to check his accuracy in relating the comet to other heavenly bodies. His friend William Lower, from Wales, sent him notes of his observations. Harriot examined them carefully, and compared them to his own findings and those of other friends who were doing the same thing. His notes still exist, some on Lower's letters and others on the margins of his own observations. The comet of 1607, as well as his correspondence with Johannes Kepler in Prague, stimulated Tom to spend more time applying his optical theories to studying the heavens.

Much later, Harriot's comet observation paid an odd dividend. Almost two centuries later, in 1784, an Austrian Harrioteer named Baron Franz von Zach, who discovered numerous Harriot papers (and mixed them up so badly that modern Harrioteers find it difficult to forgive him), printed a few of the comet notes in his astronomical journal. A young apprentice in an import-export firm, Friedrich Wilhelm Bessel, read them and calculated the orbit of the comet of 1607, using ingenious mathematics. In 1804 he sent his calculations to the German astronomer H. W. M. Olbers who appreciated the mathematical originality and encouraged the young man. Olbers even had his work published in the scientific journal *Monatliche Korrespondenz*. From this the young apprentice was offered a place at the astronomical observatory at Lilienthal, quit his job, and eventually became one of the foremost astronomers of his time. Bessel later, while working with some of Keppler's unsolved problems, invented the Bessel function, a basic tool of mathematical physics. He is best known for making the first convincing determination of the long-sought stellar parallax.

The Telescope

The telescope, which Tom called a "perspective truncke" and Galileo called a "cannon," was a new, revolutionary invention in the early 1600s. Astronomers could see surprising detail in the heavenly bodies, and spent time watching, measuring, drawing details, and otherwise learning more about objects in the sky which had long been observed by the naked eye. Mapping the heavens had been done for centuries; planets had been watched in their travels with great curiosity and care. But with a telescope celestial objects appeared brighter, as if they were closer, and could be seen in much greater detail.

Mapping the Moon

The moon was of great interest to Tom because of its influence on tides. Using his crude perspective truncke on July 26, 1609, at 9 P.M., he made the first astronomical drawing done of the moon with the aid of a telescope. The instrument was a six diameter glass, yielding an image six times larger than is seen without a telescope. He could see only one quarter of the moon at a time. Even with this handicap he started mapping the moon's surface very soon afterward, on August 5, 1609. He had wasted no time. Since Tom did not have a wife and family, he could spend almost every night observing and mapping the moon and stars with his instruments. Tom's observations of the moon continued for years, for it is a relatively easy target in clear weather. We know, too, that he shared his discoveries with his scientific colleagues.

Harriot map of the full moon

Modern photograph of the full moon

Harriot's Oxford friend and colleague William Lower lived in Llanfihengel abercomer Cairmerthen, Wales, and they regularly exchanged observations and ideas. Kit Tooke had made him a perspective cylinder, and Lower asked for several more. He shamefacedly admitted that he had not paid Tooke for the first instrument. He knew that his credit was good, however.

Lower described his first telescopic look at the moon "like the Description of Coasts in the dutch books of voyages." The full moon, he wrote, "looks like a tarte that my Cooke made me last Weeke—here a vaine of bright stuff, and there of darke, and so confusedlie all over."

Tom's lack of interest in publicity was known to his friends. They tried to get him to publish his observations and findings. In Italy, Galileo was skillful in inviting attention to his activities and in attracting honors and support from royalty and institutions. As a result, his name and his excellent work were well known outside his own country. Harriot was much more interested in learning for its own sake, although his research was equally noteworthy.

In the same letter in which he described his first telescopic view of the moon, Lower wrote, "Let your countrie and frends injoye the comforts they would have in the true and great honor you would purchase your selfe by publishing your choise workes." But Lower and Tom's other friends could do little to persuade him.

In the third century B.C. the Greek astronomer Aristarchus of Samos maintained that the earth rotates on its axis, and that it revolves around the sun. He also devised a method of estimating the distance of the sun and moon from the earth by the angle formed by them when the moon was at first or third quarter. He did this, of course, without a telescope.

Modern astronomers suspect that Harriot used one of his clearest sketches of the moon to investigate Aristarchus' findings with the aid of a telescope. Although Aristarchus' geometric model is correct in principle, the difficulty of determining the exact moment of the half-phase of the moon makes verifying the relative distances of the sun and the moon extremely difficult. Harriot's

Harriot half moon drawing and notes made at Syon April 9, 1562

sketch shows details of moon craters clearly, for shadows were created by the angle of the sun's light. The accompanying notes show how carefully Harriot was trying to determine exactly when the face of the moon was half illuminated. In the notes to this drawing, Harriot's humanity is seen at the last, 12:30 line: "Unsensibly differing. So we departed to bed."

Jupiter

After he learned that Galileo had seen Jupiter's four satellite moons with what Galileo called his cannon, Harriot reported to his friends his own first observation of Jupiter and its satellite moons. They were easily observed from Tom's garret with his perspective trunckes. At first he saw only one moon, but later observations showed the others.

Sunspots

The Aristotelian theory of perfection in the heavens did not permit any imperfections on the surface of the sun. We now know that sunspots are associated with extraordinarily complicated disturbances of the sun's atmosphere which can cause magnetic disturbances on earth. These active regions on the sun also influence the aurora borealis, or northern lights, making it possible, at times, to see the aurora as far south as Florida.

One night while visiting at Syon, Sir William Lower and Tom spent an entire night watching Jupiter and its moons. Just as the sun was coming over the horizon on Saturday, December 8, 1610, Tom saw through the frost and mist that there were spots on the rising sun. He checked with his other eye, as did Lower, and before the sun became too bright both he and Lower were convinced that there were indeed spots on the rising sun. This independent observation, checked by a colleague, of a celestial body that had been considered perfect was of great importance. Once again Aristotle's ideas were shown to be wanting. But Tom was reluctant to report on his observations of the sun, perhaps for fear of persecution.

The sun has the advantage of being visible during the day. But it can be dangerous if looked at directly, leading to loss of sight. Tom overcame this potential handicap by making his sightings in the early morning when the sun could be observed low over the misty Thames or through light clouds. He rarely made observations of the sun at midday, unless light clouds were available to dim the sunlight.

Even though he knew better, he was once careless with his sight. He observed sunspots with his naked eye, under what he noted as "fayer" (fair) conditions, and found that his sight was dim for an hour afterwards. He knew he had to be careful to avoid blindness. There is no evidence that Tom relied on the use of smoked or colored lenses to dim the sun's brightness. He knew that the glass used was often of poor optical quality and might cause flawed observations.

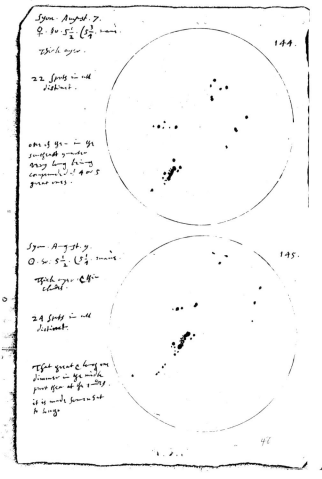

August 7 sighting, many sunspots

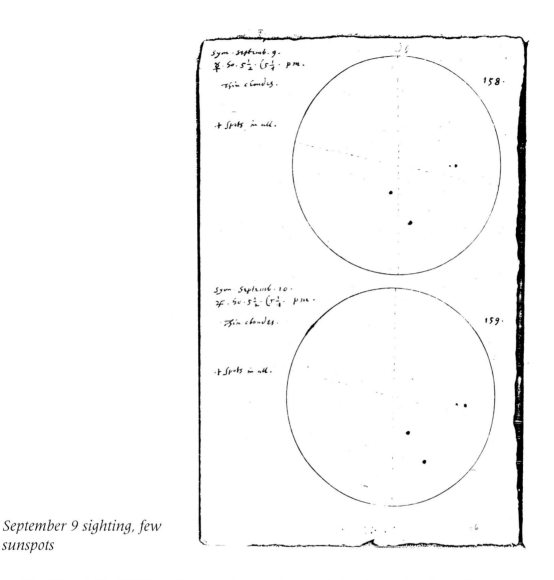

September 9 sighting, few sunspots

His friend Sir William Lower dropped out of the investigation of sunspots and returned home to Wales, but Tom kept doggedly at work. He rose every morning before sunrise to ascertain whether the early morning mist would permit an observation. If it was too clear, he returned in the late afternoon or at sunset to check the clouds and to record any visible spots. His records show that he used different perspective glasses. As his observations came to a close, he had selected two as the most useful—an instrument of ten power and one of twenty power.

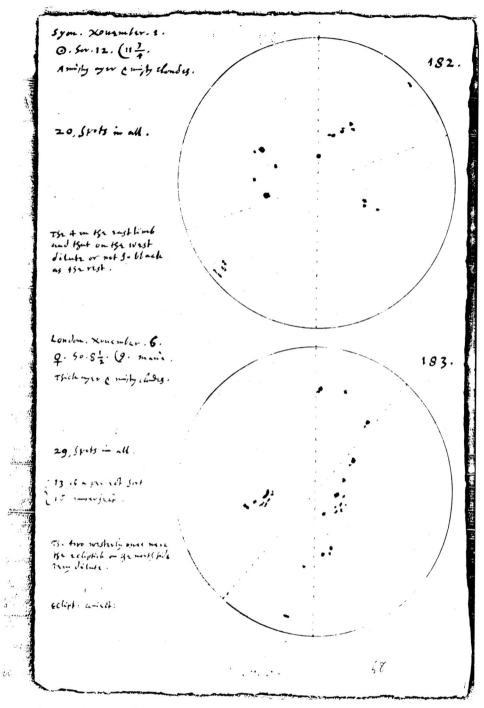

November 1 sighting, more sunspots

He made almost two hundred drawings of the solar surface, and in his notes there are four hundred and fifty separate observations. Since he was at the mercy of the weather, this was an extraordinary number to record. Most of his observations were made at Syon, but when he traveled to London, he continued them. Although he dated his drawings and noted details carefully, after June 22, 1611, he saved a few seconds of his time and no longer recorded the year in which the drawing was made.

Tom noted several different kinds of changes in sunspots. He watched new sunspots as they were generated, as they grew, as they decayed, and as they changed in intensity, as well as local movements within groups of sunspots and edge effects. And he did this by direct observations under misty conditions! Even so, his drawings were precise, as can be seen in the accompanying illustrations.

Astronomers, even today, have used Harriot's drawings. In 1978 Richard Herr used modern computer methods to determine the sun's rotation period in 1612—the earliest such determination from sunspot observations.

Observations of the changing universe have a special character that appeals to those who want to add to our knowledge of astronomy. The universe is not subject to laboratory experiment and can only be observed. Therefore someone with better equipment in a later generation cannot repeat earlier observations if they are of a phenomenon subject to change with time.

An astronomer who is interested in the changing behavior of the sun must depend upon those who kept records in previous generations. From Harriot's one hundred ninety-nine drawings of the sun, Richard Herr found that the sun rotated slightly more slowly during the first telescopically observed sunspot cycle in 1612 than in a twenty-five-day period typical of the sun today. While the drawings might seem relatively crude by modern standards, Harriot's work is still useful today.

CHAPTER 11

Problem Solving

THESE OTHER THINGS WERE ALSO HAPPENING
> 1607 · *The union of England and Scotland was rejected by the English Parliament.*
> 1608 · *Samuel de Champlain founded a French settlement in Quebec.*
> 1616 · *Galileo was prohibited by the Catholic Church from doing any further scientific work.*
> 1617 · *The Dutch bought Goree Island, off the Cape Verde Islands, from its inhabitants. It was destined to become a holding center for slaves before they were shipped overseas.*

Alchemy

Alchemy did not disappear in Tom Harriot's time. It had dominated learning for many centuries, and many people continued to believe in it. For the most part, alchemy was religious, for it aimed at the unification of all nature, under God. But there were less-than-honest alchemists, too. The signs of a fraudulent alchemist were his itinerant life (he moved around a lot) and his willingness to talk. True alchemists spent their lives in their laboratories and were very secretive. They despised the tricksters who made unbelievable claims.

Although Harriot was not enthusiastic about alchemy, he thought it might be useful to try to find the philosophers' stone. He used some experimental procedures with the properties of the four ancient elements—earth, fire, water, and air. He heated various substances in sealed glass flasks, starting with low heat and increasing the heat until the contents of the flask glowed.

At first he found that the flasks broke before he had transmuted the contents. In order to protect the glass vessels he smeared the bases with a kind of fire clay. Then he slowly heated and cooled earth (terra), water (aqua), air (aer), mercury, sulfur, and other substances, always observing and recording his observations carefully. The results were never satisfactory according to alchemical expectations, for he could not convert substances into gold. Tom eventually lost interest in pursuing the philosophers' stone.

Specific Gravity

Tom became interested in the specific gravity of various liquids and substances. He weighed, measured, and used a hydrostatic balance to determine with great accuracy the specific gravity of many things around him. The hydrostatic balance enabled him to weigh, in water, objects such as (in Harriot's spelling) his "crystall cone; grey marble octagonal, round; round lodestone of

HARRIOT'S OBSERVATIONS		MODERN READINGS	
Aurum	19.135	Gold	19.3–19.00
Argentum Vivum	13.554	Quicksilver	14.193
Plumbum nigrum	11.351	Lead (black)	11.344
Argentum	10.529	Silver	10.492
Bismutum	9.755	Bismuth	9.78–9.86
Aes	8.795	Bronze	8.80
Orichalcum	8.529	Brass	8.47–8.86
Ferrum	7.757	Iron	7.86
Chalbys	7.785	Steel	7.76–7.87
Stannum	7.297	Tin	7.76–7.87
Aqua	1.000	Water	1.00
Crystallum	2.650	Fused Quartz	2.20

Adrian Gilbert's mine; stalkes of tobacco; ashes of eggs without shells; Rubyes; Diamonds; Brown mortar; White mortar; my square amber; slag or iron; copper ore; lead ore; shoe horne; and Brimstone." A comparison of his findings and modern readings shows how accurate his specific gravity findings were.

Although Harriot expected to write a great book about the specific gravity and other characteristics of all known substances, he went back to his optical experiments.

Distillation

A sidelight of his visits to Ralegh and Northumberland in the Tower of London was its distillation house, built in 1607. Ralegh was interested in potions and medicines and was frequently called upon to treat sufferers of various illnesses with them. He often used the still to produce the potions. Henry Taylor, Clerk of the Kitchen, recorded that the still cost £20, 9s, 5d. In addition to its medicinal use, the distillation of *usquebaugh* in the Tower was mentioned in prisoners' letters as late as 1616. The modern English word for the Gaelic *usquebaugh* is whiskey.

Ballistics

Tom's ability to use his mathematical skills and his common sense as well in analyzing everyday situations were called into play by his friends and patrons. Ralegh, especially, put questions to him about fairly commonplace problems. Some were easy to answer, but others took almost a lifetime to solve. One of these lifetime projects was the way projectiles behave in the air.

From their early days at sea, both Walter Ralegh and Tom Harriot had been concerned about the behavior of projectiles shot from cannons. Warships' cannons were inaccurate unless they were fired at point-blank range. During the battle against the Spanish Armada in 1588, English vessels could maneuver close to the great Spanish galleons and hit them. But on the open sea, a barrage from a distance of more than two hundred yards was wasted.

Sixteenth-century cannons were not standardized. The heaviest were muzzle-loaded and were nicknamed "ship killers." Smaller breech-loading "man killers" were also quite various: stubby "pot guns" were the pattern for the later mortars; "demi-cannons" had nine-foot barrels and six-inch bores. They could shoot a thirty-two pound round shot of about five hundred yards, but they were not very accurate, as everyone concerned with warfare at the time knew.

Over the years Tom studied all the ancient and modern research on the problem. He listed all the possible causes of error: the quality of the gunpowder; its wetness or dryness; the weight of the ball; how it was rammed into the barrel; and the nature of the wadding that compressed the powder. He looked at other variables such as the heat of the firing piece, its movement before and after the firing, and the cleanliness of the insides of the barrel. Finally, he decided that the trajectory of the bullet or cannonball was the important, unique factor.

He drew the old Aristotelian-based circular trajectory and then applied numerical ratios between forward motion and vertical motion at different random lines. He described the nature of the flight of a projectile from the initial explosive force to the time it reached its highest point and then its descent. He was finally convinced, and others eventually agreed, that the course of a projectile must be a parabola.

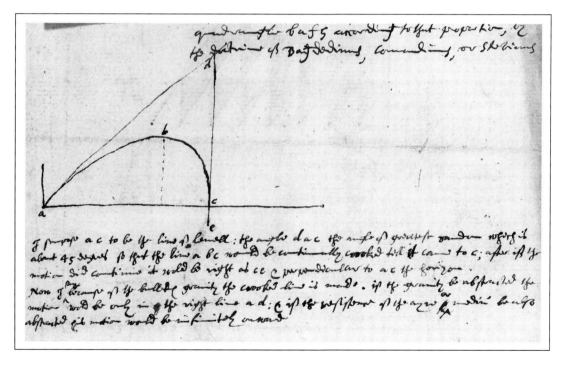

Harriot's drawing of a parabola and notes on parabolic motion

Prison

November 1605 was a tumultuous time in London, and for Tom, too. On November 5, Guy Fawkes was thought to have attempted to blow up the Parliament building, and King James was convinced that the conspirators were trying to kill him as he was to make his speech at the opening of Parliament. Since Northumberland's brother, Thomas Percy, was directly implicated, the king imprisoned the earl of Northumberland on suspicion and had Ralegh questioned. Even Tom went to the Gatehouse Prison for a time, until he petitioned for release and was granted his freedom.

The Syon Water System

Except when he visited Ralegh and Northumberland at the Tower, Tom's time back at Syon was his own. It was his his patrons' generosity that made his experimenting possible, and he was able to return his largesse, in part, by designing a water system for the Syon estate. He had long been interested in water flow and pressure and drew a rough sketch of the conduits in the system. It carried water from a spring to the stables, to the main house (where Northumberland's wife, Lady Dorothy, had the rare luxury of a private interior bath for her comfort), the laundry, and to Tom's own house.

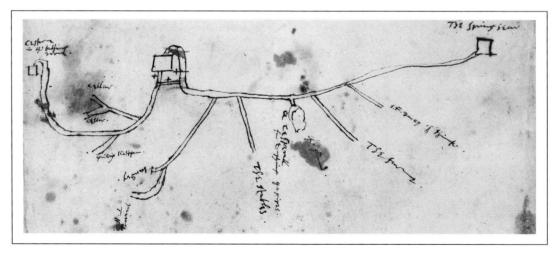

Rough sketch of the Syon water system

Billiards and Bowls

Toward the end of his life, Harriot returned to the study of how objects like bowling balls behaved when striking one another at an angle. He called it "theories of the oblique impact of elastic spheres." The earl of Northumberland, Henry Percy, had bowling greens and an indoor billiard table and was much interested in how billiard and bowling balls behaved.

A nine-page manuscript entitled *De reflexione corporum rotundorum Poristica duo* is preserved at Petworth House, and a copy is at the British Library. The 1619 paper was meticulously written (probably copied) in Latin and apparently addressed to the earl. Since this is one of the few *finished* Harriot documents, over the years it has been read by many historians of science.

Harriot considered the problem a *porism*, capable of innumerable solutions. His account did not include experimental evidence, for he called it a preliminary account, and it was purely mathematical. A modern mathematician, Johannes Lohne, analyzed the 1619 paper and asked, "What has Harriot achieved in this tract?" He answered himself, "He explained everything that can be observed when two balls rebound from each other, not only in direct, but also in oblique collision. Furthermore, he obtained remarkable results when the balls were unequal . . ."

In his short preface, Harriot presented his porisms as guides to the inner chambers or sanctuaries of nature. Lohne further suggests that in his paper "Harriot had dealt with collisions between a very small ball and a large one. His porisms show that in such cases the angle of reflection equals the angle of incidence, just as they do when alpha particles rebound from heavy atomic nuclei."

More importantly, Harriot's ideas precursed work on collisions of electrons, neutrons, and photons. In many ways, Thomas Harriot was far ahead of his time.

CHAPTER 12

What Manner of Man Was He?

THESE OTHER THINGS WERE ALSO HAPPENING

    1620 · *The Pilgrim Fathers left Plymouth in the* Mayflower *for North America.*

    1621 · *The Dutch West Indies Company was chartered; it later acquired title to the North American coast from Chesapeake Bay to Newfoundland.*

    1621 · *Potatoes were planted for the first time in Germany. They were to become a staple food in much of northern Europe.*

    1621 · *Johannes Kepler's* The Epitome of the Copernican Astronomer *was banned by the Catholic Church.*

We can only wonder what Tom Harriot thought about himself. We will never know. Some called him an "Atheist, jugler, anti-Christian hellish Aristotelian" but at the same time a friend called him the "Master of all essential and true knowledge." His enemies looked upon him with suspicion; his colleagues and friends respected him.

Thomas Harriot, 1620

The Evidence

What Tom thought about himself or others cannot be inferred from his research notes and observations, for he rarely showed himself as a person in them. A bit of verse in his lecture notes suggests that he might have had a sense of humor, as does his being called a "jugler" (entertainer or magician) by his enemies.

When in 1603 he noted the titles of books that referred to him and his work, we might believe that he wanted to prove to himself that he was well-regarded for his accomplishments. He collected this list while his friend Ralegh was in prison and in mortal danger, and Harriot's own scientific work was dormant. This might suggest that at that time his feelings affected not only in his work, but also his thoughts about his own worth. He also might have feared that he also would be imprisoned. He was a loner, spending much time with his observations and calculations. Yet he played cards with Ralegh and Northumberland, perhaps not only as a social duty that could not be avoided, but also for the joy of exercising his ability to deal with mathematical probabilities.

There is evidence that when in London he was sociable, and that he walked in St. Paul's churchyard to exchange the gossip of the day with his friends. (It was there in 1611 that John Chamberlain sought news of the ninth earl of Northumberland.) Since there were no telephones, newspapers, radio, or television for the dissemination of information, perhaps these strolls were necessary if he was to keep up with the doings of the time.

Gossip has always been a dangerous source of facts. Harriot's friends at Oxford "remembered" things many years after they occurred. A collector of information about distinguished Englishmen, John Aubrey, found out nothing about Harriot from his friends or from the records, but nevertheless invented a coat of arms for the Harriot "family." Since Tom never married and had only a few known distant relations, this family was false.

John W. Shirley, during his lifelong study of Harriot, found no public records or church records of baptism or membership for any Thomas Harriot. In 1691, however, historian Anthony à Wood found some solid evidence—Harriot's Oxford matriculation record, a one-line entry which reads: "1577, 20 Dec. St. Mary H. Hariet, Thomas; Oxon pleb.f.17."

These bare facts tell us when he was admitted, to which school, his name, birthplace (either the city of Oxford or Oxfordshire), and that his father was a plebeian (and therefore had no coat of arms). His age on this matriculation record, seventeen, is the only evidence we have been able to find about the year of his birth. There is no birth record in any of the local churches. A study of other students' matriculation records reveals that seventeen was the average age of entrance into Oxford at the time.

This tells us nothing about how Tom Harriot felt about himself. As a plebeian, we can guess that he could have felt somewhat insecure among the sons of nobles at the university. But since he was one of three in his class who eventually graduated, this is unlikely. He must have had the intellect to hold his own at Oxford. We know that he never showed concern about fine clothes. His thoughts were of more important things.

To modern eyes, Tom's friendship with Ralegh has a slight appearance of servanthood. But Ralegh trusted Harriot with very important responsibilities—training his captains in the complexities of mathematical navigation, helping to organize his Irish estates, and keeping his extensive and complex financial records. These were not the function of a household servant. In addition, Harriot's rooms at Durham House adjoined those of Ralegh. They were not in the servants' quarters. Harriot must have considered himself intellectually competent, and his patron must have agreed.

Tom Harriot's intelligence was obvious to his teachers and friends early in life. His curiosity about the world and his ability to deal with mathematical and scientific concepts, not to mention his linguistic and literary ideas, were evident to Richard Hakluyt and the principals of St. Mary's Hall, Richard Pygott and Thomas Philipson, who recommended him to the ambitious Walter Ralegh.

Another of Harriot's strengths, probably fostered at Oxford, was his purposeful historical research on the problems he encountered. That he traced classical and Arab scholarship about mathematics and navigation is a matter of record; he did the same with other projects.

He was also persistent. His regiments, as he called the mathematical and astronomical tables he calculated, required prodigious labor, for to produce them he used only his quill pens, homemade ink, and his arithmetic and mathematical abilities. That he completed most of his regiments is in itself noteworthy.

But he did not always finish what he started. His interest flagged when he saw that he was moving toward a dead end. Sometimes he was stimulated to work in another field by Ralegh or Northumberland, or by information he received of a new discovery by one of his colleagues.

One of the troublesome problems that a Harrioteer faces is Tom's habit of returning to work on a topic years after dropping it. This is complicated by his mostly undated notes. Tom's study of ballistics was probably encouraged by Ralegh as a practical problem for his privateer captains, later for the defense against the Spanish Armada, and even later as a mathematical problem confounded by Aristotelian thinking. His recurrent work in optics is another example of his working in an area for several different reasons.

Perhaps this skipping around was a strength. When he reached a mental or procedural stone wall, he temporarily stopped work. But he did not dismiss the problem from his mind. Years—sometimes decades—later he would return to the problem and attack it once more.

Publication Problems

Historians find it unfortunate that Harriot did not publish his scientific results. No doubt this has cost his reputation dearly, for he is still virtually unknown to modern mathematicians and scientists. It would be wrong to suggest that he did not care about his personal fame; his listing of the works published between 1587 and 1602 that mentioned him suggests that at the time he compiled it he was interested in his professional reputation.

Despite the fact that other scientists published their ideas and findings while he did not, most of Harriot's scientific contemporaries knew the details of his work. This might be another reason for his lack of concern for publishing his results. His correspondence and conversations with scientific leaders of his day might have made publishing seem to him a troublesome and superfluous chore. Making arrangements with a printer and preparing complex manuscripts for a compositor who would ask many questions about the material and mathematical format were not easy tasks and he had more important things to do.

Today, it is difficult for us to believe that he could disregard scholars outside his personal circle. Even in the sixteenth century, Sir William Lower wrote Harriot urging him to get his important ideas into print. Other friends did the same, but Tom Harriot was always too busy to listen to them.

There is little doubt that he had another concern. Scientists of Harriot's era were in danger of persecution and even death if the authorities found their ideas dangerous to the established beliefs. This was real and not imagined. He did not have the freedom to think and write as he wished.

In his correspondence with Johannes Kepler, Harriot said that in England he was not as free to theorize on the doctrine of the vacuum as was Kepler, since "we still stick in the mud." He said he hoped "that God would soon put an end to such nonsense." Probably he meant that complete intellectual freedom did not exist in England, but that he had hopes for the future.

Last Illness

Tom's painful last illness, a cancer of the inside of his nose, was treated by King James's own physician, Sir Theodore Turquet de Mayerne, who reported in his notes that Harriot's affliction first manifested itself in 1613. Soon after his diagnosis, Dr. Mayerne had to attend to the last illness of Queen Anne, and the king himself was bedridden. Harriot had to change doctors.

An outstanding young physician, Dr. Alexander Read, who was at the height of his fame, was called in to treat Harriot. Knowledge about the treatment of his cancer was limited, and as a last painful resort Dr. Read used cauterization with lye, even though he was not certain that it would cure Tom.

People did not live very long in Harriot's day. During his last years, he lost many of his friends. On November 6, 1612, his student Prince Henry, the heir apparent to the throne, died suddenly. Another young favorite of Harriot's, Sir John Harington, who had shared serious mathematical books and had observed the stars with him, died sixteen days later. In 1615, his close friend Sir William Lower died suddenly in Carmarthenshire, Wales. Sir Walter Ralegh was beheaded on October 21, 1618, with Harriot present. His human world was shrinking.

Last Will Revelations

Only two actual publications can be attributed to Thomas Harriot. The Virginia report was the first, and his last will and testament was the second. It was in his will that he inadvertently shared some of his innermost thoughts. He knew that he was near the end of his life and dictated the will three days before his death. It came closer to being a personal document than any of his other notes or observations.

The will also reflects his careful working habits, his attention to detail, and his clear mind just before his death. He bequeathed his belongings to those who would appreciate them. His patron, the earl of Northumberland, was willed Tom's most precious maps, charts, and his best perspective truncke, as well as the earl's choice of any books and papers.

Sir John Harington's papers, which had been placed on exhibit in a place of honor in Harriot's parlor, went to Harrington's relative by marriage Sir Robert Sidney, who had married Dorothy Percy, Northumberland's eldest daughter. Each of the executors, John Protheroe, Thomas Aylesbury, the young Viscount Lisle, and Tom Buckner, were to receive one perspective truncke and "a piece of the best glass." Harriot showed proper deference by asking Viscount Lisle to serve as an executor "if he would take pains to do so."

His servant and assistant Christopher Tooke was to get the largest cash bequest, £100, and the remainder of Tom's perspective trunckes as well as the rest of the cases, fittings, and glasses.

We learn more about Harriot's relatives from the will than from any other documents. He left his sister's son, Thomas Yates, £50 "towards the payment of his debts, but if there is anything left after the settlement of his debts, he may keep the remainder." This was an oblique comment on Thomas Yates's financial sagacity.

Another £50 was left to "John Harriottes, Late servant to Mr Doleman of Shawe neere Newberry in Barkshire, the son of my Uncles John Harriottes but now married and dwelling in Church peene about a Myle westward from the said Shawe." These are the only relatives ever mentioned in the records of the times, even though Harrioteers have searched diligently.

No wife or children were named, although in the 1689 official census of the more than 150 English settlers in Ireland, there is an entry that states "Thomas Harriot, gent. *and his family* lived on the Abbeyhouse of Molanna." It has been suggested that a census taker added the "family" to the census to inflate Ralegh's colonial efforts. There is no other evidence that Harriot was other than a lifelong bachelor.

We know from the number of household servants who were left bequests that Harriot, although a commoner and without inheritance, lived comfortably and was a generous master. He made bequests to six servants, including two who had retired. John Sheller was left £5 and the forty shillings Harriot had kept safe for him. The forty shillings were gifts given Sheller from time to time by Harriot's visiting friends. Since there were no banks for small savings accounts, Master Harriot was asked to keep the money safely for Sheller. Harriot was scrupulously honest, and remembered this small debt even on his deathbed. It is no wonder that Ralegh trusted him with much greater amounts.

Another servant, Joanne, was also left £5. Joanne's assistant, Jane, was provided 40s. The pound equaled 20s. Since Jane's wages were 20s. per year, this provides us with an estimate of the value of English money in Harriot's time as well as a sample of his generosity. Two retired servants were also remembered. Christopher Kellet was left £5 and Joanne, wife of Paul Chapmen, 40s.

His debts were few: medicines from Mr. Mayerne's "a Potycarie" and Mr. Wheatley's "a Potycarie." There was also an account with his brewer, dwelling at Brantford End, and to "Mr. John Bill, Stacioner for Bookes." He estimated that the total of all these debts was more or less £40. After his debts were paid, £20 was to go to the poor.

The considerate Harriot, in order to repay Tom Buckner's wife, in whose house he lay dying, left her £15 for her trouble. Buckner's son, with whom Tom had often spoken, received £5. Buckner himself was a well-to-do merchant and was an executor of his estate; he received no cash bequest.

Memorialized

Tom Buckner wrote in his journal on July 1, 1621: "Today my old friend Thomas Harriot died. At last he is at peace. He will be buried in St. Christopher's

Parish Church, of which I am a vestryman, tomorrow. A Memorial to Thomas Harriot will be erected in the chancel of the choir east of the nave."

It is, appropriately, in Latin but may be translated:

> *Stay, traveler, lightly tread*
> *Near this spot lies all that was mortal*
> *Of that most celebrated man*
> *THOMAS HARRIOT.*
> *He was that most learned Harriot*
> *of Syon on the River Thames;*
> *By birth and education*
> *An Oxonian*
> *Who cultivated all the sciences*
> *And excelled in all—*
> *In Mathematics, Natural Philosophy, Theology*
> *A most studious searcher after truth*
> *A most devout worshipper of the Triune God*
> *At the age of sixty or thereabouts,*
> *He bade farewell to mortality, not to life.*
> *The Year of our Lord 1621, July 2.*

Although the church was burned down in the great London fire of 1666, the wording of the memorial was preserved and is now included in a brass plaque located in the entrance hall of the Bank of England in London.

AFTERWORD

BY NECESSITY, MOST OF THE SCIENTIFIC TOPICS in this book are not treated in depth. If he were still living, Tom Harriot would be the first to encourage you, when you become curious about a question, to find out more. The library, laboratory, and observatory are good places to start.

I hope that you now want to know more about Thomas Harriot himself and his colleagues. Although very little is really known about many of them, there are several ways a truly interested Harrioteer can proceed. Excellent books are often available in good research libraries, and some are still for sale in bookstores.

The most comprehensive resource is that of John W. Shirley, *Thomas Harriot: A Biography* (Oxford: Oxford University Press, 1983). Shirley includes valuable leads to other materials about Harriot and his colleagues which he has consulted over the years. The bibliography is divided into three periods: materials that date from 1580 to 1700, from 1700 to 1900, and since 1900.

The earliest group includes "Primary Harriot Manuscripts and Signatures" and "Secondary Manuscript References to Harriot," specifying the places where the items can be found, usually libraries, castles, and public record offices. These are primary Harriot sources, and usually very hard to find in the original.

The early "Books and References to Harriot" cataloged by Shirley include those that Harriot listed himself in 1603, as well as George Chapman's 1601

Translation of the whole work of Homer, the preface of which says that Chapman conferred only with Robert Hues and Harriot in making his translation.

The 1700–1900 references include some manuscripts collected in the nineteenth century by Stephen P. and Stephen J. Rigaud which are in the Bodleian Library at Oxford, and books and periodical articles that mention Harriot. The references published since 1900 are varied interpretations of Harriot and his contemporaries. Many of them are commented upon by Shirley in the body of his very useful biography.

In the United States, photocopies of some of Harriot's papers are available in the Special Collections Department of the University of Delaware Library in Newark, Delaware. Many of them were from Shirley's own library. An examination of these materials suggests how difficult it was for him and other scholars to track Harriot's pioneering work.

Harriot's comprehensive report on Virginia's riches is easily available. It has been reproduced from an original Library of Congress copy of the first illustrated version of the work (engravings made from John White's paintings), published by Theodore deBry in Frankfurt-am-Main in 1590. This softcovered book can be ordered from Dover Publications, New York.

The original of Harriot's only other published work, his last will and testament, is at the Guildhall Library in London. A photocopy of his will, dated 1621, is included in a useful book which has additional scientific and historical articles about Harriot from many sources: John W. Shirley, ed., *A Source Book for the Study of Thomas Harriot* (New York, Arno Press, 1981). Shirley also collected papers from a 1971 Symposium on Harriot at the University of Delaware: *Thomas Harriot, Renaissance Scientist* (Oxford: Clarendon Press, 1974).

In 1900, a book by Henry Stevens was privately published in a limited edition of thirty-three large paperback copies and 162 copies on small paper. Stevens was an amateur—a bookseller and lover of books—and his manuscript was completed in 1885. He had consulted many original Harriot manuscripts in the British Museum, and was the first to locate the last will and testament, which he copied. His book has been reprinted, and is now available in some libraries: *Thomas Harriot, the Mathematician, the Philosopher, the Scholar* (New York: Burt Franklin, 1972).

David Beers Quinn is a specialist in Tudor and Elizabethan history and Sir Walter Ralegh's activities. He has written many books, one of which was prepared for America's 400th Anniversary and relates to the exploration of the New World: *Set Fair for Roanoke. Voyages and Colonies, 1584–1606* (Chapel Hill and London: The University of North Carolina Press, 1985).

An unusual treatment of Harriot's obscure life and real contributions is Muriel Ruykeyser's poetic treatment: *The Traces of Thomas Hariot* (New York: Random House, 1971).

A comprehensive technical book on navigation which may be of interest is D.W. Waters's *The Art of Navigation in Elizabethan and Stuart Times* (New Haven: Yale University Press, 1958).

For an exciting account of the attempt by the Catholic Spanish Armada to conquer Protestant England, Garrett Mattingly's *The Armada* (Boston: Houghton Mifflin, 1959), takes the reader into the battle itself after painting the secular and religious background of the first great sea battle in history.

An example of how Harriot's work is still relevant for modern scientists is Richard Herr's article in the December 8, 1978 issue of *Science*, "Solar Rotation Determined from Thomas Harriot's Sunspot Observations of 1611 to 1613."

Potential Harrioteers can consult many other books and articles. Often, the references in the above sources will give the Harriot detective valuable clues to new evidence of Harriot's importance in the history of science.

ACKNOWLEDGMENTS

MANY INDIVIDUALS AND INSTITUTIONS have helped make this book possible. Harrioteers past and present too numerous to mention have kept alive the memory of Thomas Harriot. Some of the sources in the Afterword will lead you to them. In addition, institutions that have collected materials related to Harriot over the years have been generous in sharing materials for illustrations.

The late John W. Shirley, who encouraged me to write of Thomas Harriot and his times, deserves full credit for being a motivating force. The comments and suggestions of his colleagues at the University of Delaware, such as George Basalla, Professor of History of Science, and the librarians in the Special Collections Department of the University of Delaware Library, Timothy Murray, Rebecca Johnson, and Gary E. Yela, have been most helpful. Professor of Mathematics Robert M. Stark of the University of Delaware and Newark High School mathematics teacher Kathy Williams read the mathematics chapters and made useful suggestions. Professor Richard Herr of the Department of Physics and Astronomy at the University of Delaware was generous and patient in helping a nonastronomer understand important concepts in that field and to help the reader avoid misconceptions in all fields.

Many of the ideas in the "These Other Things Were Happening" sections at the beginning of most chapters were adapted from Bernard Grun's *The Timetable of History* published in 1991 by Simon & Schuster. This book is a direct translation from the German of Werner Stein's *Kulturfahrplan.*

Julie Rickerman, former librarian of the Ralph C. Staiger Library of the International Reading Association, was especially helpful in locating institutions and materials. Larry Husfelt, graphic designer for the International Reading Association, provided much help with the illustrations.

Special thanks are due to my daughter, Joan Marie Staiger, for her many suggestions and proofreading and to my wife, Marian, for her patience throughout the years I have been a Harrioteer.

Permission to Use Illustrations

The illustrations in this book came from many sources, and permission to use them is gratefully acknowledged from these institutions and individuals: The Thomas Harriot portrait used as the frontispiece is reproduced with the permission of the President and Fellows of Trinity College, Oxford, together with a reminder that there is no solid evidence that it is authentic. The Queen Elizabeth I engraving is from a copy in the North Carolina Collection, University of North Carolina, Chapel Hill. The Ralph Aggas Map of Oxford, 1578, is in the Bodleian Gough Maps Collection, Oxford University. *The Boyhood of Raleigh* by John E. Millais, 1870, is in the Tate Gallery, London. Permission to reproduce was obtained through Art Resource, 65 Bleecker Street, New York. Sir Humphrey Gilbert's portrait is from the Ashmolean Museum, Oxford. The Sir Richard Grenville portrait engraving is from a copy in the North Carolina Collection, University of North Carolina Library, Chapel Hill. The *Tiger* sketch was provided by the National Maritime Museum, London. The sketch of The *Golden Hind* is reproduced by permission of Longman Education, from the *Then and There Series —Elizabethan Ship*, 1956. Captain John Davis's 45° Backstaff of 1595 is from *The Seaman's Secrets* 1657, a reprint of the 1595 edition by courtesy of the Whitehall Library of the Ministry of Defense, London. Similarly, Captain John Davis's "Layout of a Logbook" of 1593 is from *The Seaman's Secrets* 1657, a reprint of the 1595 edition by courtesy of the Whitehall Library of the Ministry of Defense, London. The photograph of the Ensign

Global Positioning System was provided by courtesy of Trimble Navigation. The Rare Book and Special Collections of the Library of Congress granted permission to use the illustrations in the Theodore DeBry 1590 edition of *A Briefe and True Report of the New Founde Land of Virginia* which Lessing Rosenwald presented to the Library of Congress. This includes the engravings made from the John White paintings made in 1585. The Oxford University Press authorized the Algonquian renditions of "Manteo" and "Wanchese" in Harriot's phonetic alphabet, taken from Shirley's *Thomas Harriot*. Harriot's phonetic alphabet is reproduced with permission from the British Library. The John Dee portrait is from the British Museum. The Northwest Passage map prepared for Sir Humphrey Gilbert by John Dee is from the Rare Book Department of the Free Library of Philadelphia. The title page of the 1588 edition of *A Briefe and True Report of the New Founde Land of Virginia* is reproduced by permission of the British Library. The portrait of the ninth earl of Northumberland by Van Dyke is in the Petworth Collection of the National Trust and is reproduced courtesy of the Right Honorable Lord Egremont and the National Trust. The sketch of Glover's plan of Syon, 1635, is reproduced by courtesy of His Grace, the Duke of Northumberland. The moon drawings by Harriot are from the Petworth Papers of the University of Delaware Library, Special Collections Department. They are reproduced by permission of Lord Egremont. The photograph of the full moon is from Professor Richard Herr's personal collection. The Harriot drawings of sunspots, numbers 144–45, 158–59, and 182–83 are also in the Petworth Papers of the University of Delaware and are reproduced by permission of Lord Egremont. Harriot's parabolic motion sketch is in the British Library. The rough sketch of the waterworks at Syon by Harriot is from the British Library's Manuscript Collection. Thomas Harriot's 1620 portrait engraved by Francis Delaram is in the British Museum.

INDEX